Writing and Respo

C000133043

'This excellent book is invaluable for Creative Writing students. It encourages the student to question their own practice both as a writer and a reader, and asks pointed questions about the role of a writer in society.'

Julia Bell, *Birkbeck, University of London*

In a world where literary scandals often end up in court, the issue of responsibility in writing has never been so important. In this groundbreaking study, Carl Tighe asks the questions every writer needs to consider:

- What is it that writers do? Are they responsible for all the uses to which their writing might be put? Or are they no more responsible than their readers?
- How are a writer's responsibilities compromised or defined by commercial and political pressures, or by notions of tradition or originality?
- How do writers' audiences affect their responsibilities?
- Are responsibilities the same for writers in all parts of the world, under all political and social systems?

The first part of this book defines responsibility and looks at its relation to ideas such as power, accuracy, kitsch and political correctness. The second part examines how particular writers have dealt with these issues through case studies of such controversial works as *American Psycho*, *Crash* and *The Tin Drum*.

Writing and Responsibility encourages its readers to interrogate the choices they make as writers. A fascinating look at the public consequences of the private act of writing, Carl Tighe's book is a must-read for everyone who writes or studies writing.

Carl Tighe teaches Creative Writing at the University of Derby and is a successful writer of both fiction and non-fiction. His first novel, *Burning Worm*, was short-listed for the 2001 Whitbread Award and won the Authors' Club Award. His most recent publication was the novel *KssssS: A Tale of Sex, Money and Alien Invasion*.

Writing and
Responsibility

Carl Tighe

Routledge
Taylor & Francis Group

LONDON AND NEW YORK

First published 2005 by Routledge
2 Park Square, Milton Park, Abingdon, Oxon OX14 4RN

Simultaneously published in the USA and Canada
by Routledge
270 Madison Ave, New York, NY 10016

Routledge is an imprint of the Taylor & Francis Group

© 2005 Carl Tighe

Typeset in Baskerville by The Running Head Limited, Cambridge
Printed and bound in Great Britain by TJ International,
Padstow, Cornwall

British Library Cataloguing in Publication Data
A catalogue record for this book is available from the British Library

Library of Congress Cataloging in Publication Data
Tighe, Carl, 1950–
Writing and responsibility / Carl Tighe
    p. cm.
Includes bibliographical references and index.
1. Literature and morals. 2. Literature, Modern – 20th century –
History and criticism. I. Title
PN49.T47 2005
801'.3–dc22   200411715

ISBN 0–415–34562–6 (hbk)
ISBN 0–415–34563–4 (pbk)

Contents

Acknowledgements

Thanks to:

The Writers' and Translators' Centre of Rhodes; John Flower, Julian Preece, Osman Durani, Frankie Hudson and David Emerson, Norman Leach, David and Anne Downes, Jon Preece, Mary Niesłuchowska, Mariola Żychowska, Shirley Franklin, Yvonne Lyon, Cathie and Tony Gard, Mick and Pat O'Rourke, Brian Way, David Sims, John Worthen, John Turner, Wyn Thomas, Nick Potter, Roger Shipton, Pat Squires, Chris Binns, Des Smith and Corine Deliot, Nigel Jenkins, John Osmond, Ned Thomas, Duncan Bush, Jerry Roland, Allan Sennett, Alan Sinner, Sue Habeshaw, Nick Otty, Michael Hulse, Tony Rees, Moy McCrory, Simon Heywood, Liz Cashdan, Ann Atkinson, Maggie and Tim Shields, Bev Llewellyn, Linda Kempton, Rowena Edlin-White, Gerry Kreibich, Graham Sellors, Greg Heath, Colin Sutherill, Mitzi Szereto, Raymond Greenoaken, Amanda Metcalf, Steve Wetton, Brendan Murphy, Jerry Hope, Chris Thompson, Cliff Holden, Star, Madeleine and Luke Rose.

1   Introduction

This first chapter is about writing as a private act with public consequences. It looks at the history of writing, and the global, personal and ethical dilemmas writers deal with, questioning the role of the writer in contemporary society.

This chapter sees writing as 'rendering an account'. It asks what writers are responsible for, and to whom they are responsible. It also highlights some of the issues writers ask themselves about their work and explores the broad social and political concerns writers take into consideration when making artistic decisions.

> You're pleasing yourself when you're writing. You're not pleasing a bunch of other people. You're not constructing a little candy house, or a little gingerbread house that everyone can take a piece of and feel sweet and nice and that makes them feel good about themselves . . . Writing a book is actually a very selfish and very aggressive thing. You're writing this book and putting it out there and it says: Read me! Read me! Read me!
>
> (Bret Easton Ellis (Clarke 1996/98))

Rendering accounts

In the three-million-year history of the human species, writing is a relatively recent development. We can trace its origins to Stone Age tally sticks and clay tokens dating from about 8000 BC, and to cave painting, but writing proper seems to have developed only about 3500–2600 BC (Schmandt-Besserat 1992). Although many of the earliest surviving examples have yet to be deciphered, it is clear that writing is connected to palace culture, rule and order, keeping accounts, tracking stores, enabling survival. Without writing, how could we map our territories or record good hunting areas? How could we order armies to move, make laws and regulations or keep track of kinship? If making marks of some sort was originally a form of keeping accounts, and later grew into what we now call writing, and if the responsible management of stores, palaces and cities developed into what we now call civilization, why should we imagine that a connection of writing with responsibility that is so important to the species as a whole should be anything less at a personal level?

Philosophers and responsibility

Philosophers have long pondered ideas of responsibility and writing. Aristotle's *Ethics* (367–347 BC) offers a useful example of such reflections. He points out that without writing there is no government, without government there is no civilization, without civilization there is no writing. Writing is inextricably intertwined not only with individual consciousness but also with society and thus with responsibility. For Aristotle, we are all responsible for the actions in which we have a choice and awareness of the consequences of an action is the mark of a citizen. While all humans deliberate the right course of action, Aristotle argued that:

> The arts call for more deliberation than the sciences, because we feel less certain about them. Thus the field of deliberation is that which happens for the most part, where the result is obscure and the right course not clearly defined.
>
> (Aristotle 2003: 119)

Such deliberation, we might argue, is built into narrative: the selection of which 'beginning', which 'middle' and which 'ending' is as much a moral or political as an artistic decision.

If we have a moral responsibility to make the 'right' decisions, in action or in narrative, we immediately come up against the issue of authority. As long as 'the word' was the word of God there was no real crisis of authority. During the medieval period, writing had been primarily religious in purpose. For example, as indicated by titles such as *Everyman* (1508–34) or *Mankind* (*c.* 1475), plays dealt in human averages and archetypes, rather than in individual personalities, and were used to teach moral lessons. However, the authority of the Church in England was seriously weakened by the Dissolution of the Monasteries in 1536. After this, its role as the sole arbiter of moral matters and the repository of all that was known and thought started to dwindle.

The universities set up to train young men for government began to grow and prosper, at first in the shadow of the Church and then less so. With that change it became possible to think things that the Church would have disapproved of, and as a result many of the restraints upon the development of writing and theatre as art forms, entertainment and commentary on life simply disappeared. Theatre in particular moved away from its solely religious function to become entertainment and began to look at relations, changes and pressures within society in ways that had previously been impossible.

With the decay of feudalism, there grew a fantastic interest in the individual minds, capacities and abilities of men and, to a lesser extent, in those of women. The work of the new writers, some of whom were university educated, revelled in the beauty of human beings and their seemingly boundless capacity for inquiry and knowledge. Renaissance literature named individual people rather than general humanity as its theme: Marlowe's *Doctor Faustus* (*c.* 1588) or Shakespeare's *Hamlet, Macbeth* or *Coriolanus* (*c.* 1600–6) are but a few of the period's studies of the restless, inquisitive, acquisitive personal and intellectual life that was opening up for the individual. Hamlet's soliloquy about humanity, 'What a piece of work is man' (*Hamlet*, II ii 303–10), would have been unthinkable in a medieval mystery or morality play.

As writers and readers we are the inheritors of the freedoms the Renaissance won. The social changes initiated in the period removed moral authority from the Church and allowed us to become responsible for our own lives and our own choices. These social changes also gave rise to a literary culture that did not necessarily accept the narrative structures of the Bible as its only models: instead narrative began to display a moral structure that was not predetermined but deeply ambiguous and ambivalent. This might be seen as the beginning of today's uncertain, market-orientated literary culture.

Morality and writing

What then are the moral, professional, practical and artistic dilemmas facing those who now commit words to writing? Oscar Wilde, who elsewhere stated that all art is immoral, said in the preface to his 1890 novel, *The Picture of Dorian Gray* (Wilde 2003: 3) that there was no such thing as a moral or an immoral book – only badly written books. Wilde's book did offend, however, and was taken as an endorsement of a certain lifestyle, even if later critics have argued that it was at its core curiously moral in purpose. The question of immorality has more recently revealed itself in a series of highly publicized claims against films. It has been said, for example, that the films *A Clockwork Orange* and *Natural Born Killers* were both responsible for copycat attacks or killings, while Clint Eastwood's *Dirty Harry* movies have been blamed for a rise in vigilantism in the USA. Rock music lyrics have also been blamed for violent acts. In 1996 the lyrics of the rock band Slayer were cited in a California court by parents of a girl who had been killed by three boys following necrophiliac 'instructions' in a song called 'Kill Again'. The lyrics of Ozzy Osborne have also been cited in several cases of teenage suicide.

In the USA grieving parents have attempted to make musicians and song-writers responsible in law for 'causing or encouraging' death with their lyrics, only to find that artists are protected by the First Amendment to the Constitution, which guarantees freedom of speech. In the UK the impact of the European Charter on Human Rights, folded into English law as the Human Rights Act (1998), brings the right to free expression into conflict with the right to privacy and with current laws on libel and defamation in a very similar way (Boundy 2003: 10).

Fiction writers demonstrate an ongoing concern with the issue of moral responsibility, or the 'morality' of writing. It is a steady theme in the works of Angela Carter, Alice Walker, Maya Angelou, Wole Soyinka, Buchi Eme-cheta, Chinua Achebe, Ngugi Wa Thiongo and many others who write about, for example, rape or murder, poverty or racism. It is there in a whole list of scandalous literary events, from the *Lady Chatterley's Lover* trial to the furore surrounding Bret Easton Ellis's *American Psycho*, the *fatwah* pronounced against Salman Rushdie for his *Satanic Verses*, or Science Fiction's warnings about plague and genetic engineering. A concern with moral responsibility affects the choice and use of language in post-colonial and migrant writing and informs much women's, gay and lesbian writing and, after the successes of J. K. Rowling and Philip Pullman, it is clear that the issue is a part of writing for children (Pullman 2002: 4; Fine 2003: 12; Wallace 2003: 18).

Defining responsibility

Most of us have some idea about professional responsibility only in relation to medical ethics. We can point to the Hippocratic Oath, which is a convenient fiction rather than a legally binding document, since doctors do not physically take an oath, but which is nevertheless an effective statement of professional intent. If we hear of a doctor murdering elderly patients for their money we have a very clear notion that this contradicts our expectations of the medical profession. However, if we hear of a teacher having sex with a pupil or a car dealer welding together two halves of different vehicles, our reaction is rather different. Circumstances alter cases, we might argue. How old was the pupil? What did they pay for the car? Our notion of responsibility or of what is allowable within the practice of these professions is less clearly defined.

So what notion of responsibility might we possess in relation to the profession of writing? Most of us have some idea of what we mean by 'writing', but it is not a word we normally find linked with *responsibility*. English probably gets the word responsibility, via French, from the Latin word *respondere*, an obligation (literally, *re-spondere*, to promise in return). This is also the source for the English words *spouse* and *sponsor*, both of which indicate a reciprocal arrangement between two parties. The *Oxford English Dictionary*'s long list of meanings for the word touches upon such concepts as obligation, trust, duty, accountability, reliability, rational conduct, reputation and respectability. Being responsible, it seems, means being part of society, whether we want it or not, so the responsibility of the writer depends on their role in society. The theorist and writer Edward Said has elaborated the idea that writing is part of a spectrum of interconnected human activities that cannot be divorced from other aspects of our lives, and that no country is exempt from the debate about what is to be read, taught or written (Said 1993).

The South African novelist Nadine Gordimer learned that it was an act of responsibility to write:

> In my case, being born in a country like South Africa, white, automatically privileged, living, brought up in the colonial life, as I was, if I was going to be a writer there would have to be a time when I would see what was in that society, when I would see how it had shaped me and my thinking and that I would bear, automatically, a certain responsibility for it as a human being. And since a writer is an articulate human being, there would be a special responsibility to respond to it in a certain way.
>
> (Bourne *et al.* 1987: 25)

Ian Curteis, President of the Writers Guild of Great Britain, has said that, in particular, writers involved in broadcasting have a huge responsibility since their work 'has more direct influence on society, people's assumed values and the way they conduct their lives, and what they believe than any other force' (Curteis 2000: 7). However, while most writers accept that they are in some way responsible for what they write, some are surprised that anyone should think them responsible, in any way, for anything they might have said, written, thought or caused to happen. Even when writers acknowledge a responsibility forced upon them, their thoughts on the subject can be vague and unfocused. Some writers say they write to please themselves and take no heed of what anyone else might think, even in terms of pure entertainment. They might feel very little obligation to entertain, or might even consider their responsibility as writers to lie in opposing the very idea of entertainment or, for that matter, in opposing the notion of responsibility.

Those writers who acknowledge responsibilities of course differ in the specifics of how they perceive them. Some speak of social, personal, familial, professional or philosophical responsibilities; others feel responsible towards a craft or genre. They may see their responsibilities in connection with literary traditions, literary forms, markets for work, professional obligations, particular political parties, in opposition to political power, in relation to our supposed rights within the law, our freedom of speech and notions of what is correct or socially acceptable, or even in relation to the 'politically correct' or socially acceptable. W. B. Yeats, for example, wondered whether his poetry had sent men out to die fighting the English in the Easter Rising of 1916. Writers might also argue that responsibilities connected to particular literary forms might be substantially different, or that they write in conditions where responsibilities are seen and defined differently, and where the definition of a writer's responsibilities is constantly shifting. Others have split responsibilities: some writers in the former easern-bloc countries were required to be servants of the state, but also felt allegiance and therefore a responsibility to oppositionist movements.

Global and personal responsibility

Looking back over the last few years we can see from the life and work of such writers as Soviet Alexander Solzhenitsyn, Australian Thomas Keneally, Nigerians Chinua Achebe and Wole Soyinka, Anglo-Indian Salman Rushdie and the Czech writer-President Václav Havel that within the underlying problems of responsibility to one's people, ethnic group, language or nationality there is a growing sense of general political responsibility that goes far beyond the local and the immediate. Global issues and questions hang in the air for all writers, whatever their origins or loyalties.

We can define responsibilities in terms of how writers think, but we might also define responsibilities in terms of who or what (we think) the writers are: in terms of, for example, ethnic or national origin, religion or gender, sexual preference or social class, to name but a few possibilities. This means that writers, particularly when creating out of their own experience, are often very aware of the difficulties of disentangling truth and fiction, between creating a lie, no matter how grounded in autobiographical 'fact', and creating a story. Writer Jeanette Winterson has said that lies are just lies, intended to deceive others by passing as the truth, whereas what art tries to do is 'cut through all that and come up with something that really is objective' (Brooks 2000: 10).

Writers cannot help drawing upon personal experience, but if writing has the power to help us understand ourselves and our world, it also has the power to fix events, to present one side of the case, to pretend to offer 'the truth'. To take this idea further, does the idea of artistic licence allow writers to reveal secrets or details of 'real' events that might damage others? John Bayley's memoir of his wife Iris Murdoch, *Iris: A Memoir* (1998) enjoyed strong sales, but Bayley was taken to task for writing so openly about the details of his marriage to the novelist Iris Murdoch and the changes in her personality brought about by the onset of Alzheimer's disease. Critic and academic Germaine Greer has been accused of unnecessarily exposing her father's past in *Daddy, We Hardly Knew You* (1989). This single issue of creating from experience gives rise to a wide range of views around writing and responsibility, but as we shall see, there are many more questions to be asked.

The private/public act

Over the last ten years globalization – another name for the apparently irresistible rise of US commercial, political and military power – has made massive inroads into our lives and has increased our awareness of the many possible applications of the slogan 'the personal is the political'. We are much more aware of the interconnectedness of things. We worry, among many other things, that clothing retailers operating in countries like Thailand and Cambodia are breaking international labour agreements by exploiting underage, low-paid workers, toiling in sweatshop conditions to produce clothes and shoes which are sold at a massive profit in western stores.

A new awareness of the fragile state of the ecology of our planet furthers our understanding of the interconnectedness of the public and the private. That even the most apparently inconsequential act has hidden aspects is now taken for granted by many of us, even if some have resolved to respond by doing nothing and to accept the status quo. The collapse of communism, the disintegration of Yugoslavia, difficulties in post-colonial Africa, slow political reforms in China, changes facing the Catholic Church, the rise of Christian fundamentalism in the USA and the rise of Islamic fundamentalism have all forced revisions in our understanding of the nature of moral, political and religious leadership. But while the *fatwah* pronounced against Salman Rushdie for his *Satanic Verses* appears with hindsight to be a precursor to the events of 11 September 2001 and the escalation of conflict in the Middle East, those events have not made the issues of responsibility any clearer. What they have done is to make it clear only that responsibility is a global issue. Writing and writers are part of this world. Writers and their works operate in a context, and whether they wish it or not, someone somewhere will hold them responsible for what they write.

It is the potential power of the word that makes writing the subject of many conflicts. Literature can test the judgements that societies make and show up areas in our lives where political and religious leaders have failed to provide answers. In this way, its influence can be great: even the idea of writing has implications for those who seek to control writers and for those who seek, for whatever reason, to read what writers write. Politicians and religious leaders almost always seek to enlist writers to their cause or to control them, in order to limit the intellectual and popular opposition their work might arouse. At the other end of the power scale, the written word can seem vitally important to societies facing threats to the survival of their nation, identity, language or way of life.

Writing brings the public world into private scrutiny and puts private thought into the public domain. This public/private conjunction makes writing a highly political act in any society and renders the issue of responsibility highly contentious, particularly in repressive societies. South African writer André Brink has pointed out that in the USA, Britain, France, Sweden and elsewhere it is possible to ask the question, 'Surely it cannot be enough merely to write?' which implies that writing is a way of not 'doing something'. Within repressive societies, on the other hand, writing is often seen as an act 'not of turning one's back on the world but of fully immersing oneself in it' (Brink 1983: 165).

Responsibility exists when an action is committed, or when an action is omitted. Writers are constantly faced with decisions about what to write and what not to write, what to write about and what not to write about. Sometimes a state might forbid certain material: communist states are perhaps the most obvious example, but it should not be forgotten that the UK has in its Official Secrets Act one of the western world's most comprehensive, punitive and wide-ranging legislative controls over writing, publication and public debate.

So is the writer wrong to reveal 'classified information' if it seems to be in the public interest to do so, or not? How disloyal is it for a writer to point out that they do not consider the actions of their government to be respectable? The factors that determine any decision about what to write and what to write about are many and varied: individuals operate within and reflect in themselves a complex and conflicted society, where an infinite number of ideas compete for attention. Each writer embodies differing tendencies, ambitions and experiences, and in this way artistic decisions and the responsibility that goes with them are personal. However, the responsibility is also social and moral: to decide to write or not write about something in particular constitutes a response to the social and political world, and the resulting publication or broadcast is a contact with other intellects. This interaction can be traced through the history of literature, with early examples to be found in the Homeric epics and tragedies of the Greek classical world and in the life and death of Socrates (Havel 1988: 232–3, 301).

Writing does remain in one other crucial way a private activity: in most cases writers are not controlled during the actual writing process and it is only when they have produced something that it enters the public domain. Only then can control or rejection, controversy or influence come into play. In the last resort, then, we can only say that individual writers take their own decisions – to challenge or to replicate, to do or not to do – for which they and they alone are responsible. With them remains the question, 'Should I have known better?'

The role of the writer

It is hard to imagine a society where human actions are not judged in terms of responsibility and obligation – even our legal system takes into account ideas of diminished or limited responsibility, or implies a lack of rational choice in the 'absence of responsibility'. But how much real influence do writers have and how does the public view them? For some critics, writing at its finest marks a curve on the graph of social development and human consciousness. Yet, from ancient Greece right down to the present, others have dismissed writers – particularly poets – as dreamers or liars, disconnected from the 'real world'. Obviously the impact of an architect's irresponsibility should they design a house that then collapses and kills the occupants cannot be compared with the results of writing a poorly researched essay. But what of the writer who decides not to expose a matter of national security? Many writers have seen their role as crucial, at least potentially, and consequently have considered their moral responsibility to be great.

Saint Paul used poetry as a back-up in his effort to convert the people of Athens to Christianity and referred to poetry as a moral authority on a par with the prophets (Acts 17:26; Titus 1:12). The poet Shelley held the opinion that 'poets are the unacknowledged legislators of the world', by which he meant that writers of all kinds had a responsibility to observe and improve the world by exposing folly, by making people more aware of their feelings and more aware of the world around them. In a more recent example, playwright Edward Bond has said repeatedly that in the face of a rapacious modern society, a society that in his view shows very little sense of responsibility, writers do not have the luxury of getting out, and that looking to the natural world of animals only shows us that we too are savages with a gloss of civilization. Bond insists that for a writer the popular notion of 'going insane' under the pressure of modern life is not an option. For him it is the duty and responsibility of the writer to stay sane, to observe, record, comment and criticize (Bond 1995: 12).

But to what extent can we trust writers to know and tell us the truth about how we live, about the kind of creatures we are, or about how life might be better? Writer and critic Matthew Arnold (1822–88) said:

> Everyone can see that a poet, for instance, ought to know life and the world before dealing with them in poetry; and life and the world, being in modern times, very complex things, the creation of a modern poet, to be worth much, implies a great critical effort behind it; else it would be a comparatively poor, barren and short lived affair.
>
> (Arnold n.d.: 4)

Russian writer Nikolai Bukharin (1888–*c.* 1938) would probably have agreed with Arnold. Bukharin put great stress on the role intellectuals and writers – particularly poets – would have to play in the Russian Revolution and saw the tasks of both writing and revolution as improving the world. What was needed, he argued, was breadth and depth of knowledge, the ability to 'feel a thing through and through, to bring it out to the light of day, to put it into form'. However for Bukharin the level of poetic culture in his time was 'terribly low, both in its content and its formal attributes' and he could find no poets who had a sense of the 'great universal canvas' that was opening up for revolutionary artists, nor any who really felt to the full the historic place they might take in 'the living stream of modern history'. Creating a revolution was one thing. Creating a revolutionary art was another. Poet Linton Kwesi Johnson's 'Intavenshuns' have shown that public poetry can be a highly effective and responsible literary form. However, at the same time, Germaine Greer has written:

> Poetry is now a special-interest area. [. . .] The practitioners of poetry probably outnumber the readers of poetry; in the United States the number of people registered for tax purposes as poets is more than a hundred times the number of the average print-run of a book of poems. [. . .] It is not poetry but advertising that is the literary form of the late twentieth century.
>
> (Greer 1996: xii)

So can writers change the world? Probably not, but perhaps they can still try. Certainly notions of 'power' and 'authority' in creative texts and in political life have become far more problematic within the liberal democracies of the west over the past fifty years. Do electors really surrender power to politicians? Do readers really surrender themselves up to authors? Are readers the real writers? The lines have become blurred. There is no general agreement that writing has any role either in maintaining current power structures, or in offering any serious challenge to them. The withdrawal of censorship in virtually the entire area of written and visual culture might be seen as an indicator that the written word is no longer a site of major debate or negotiation about change. But if writers and writing cannot change the world, they can at least help improve it inch by inch.

Whatever their power, writers seem to occupy an unusual place in human society, often ignored or vilified, rarely praised and cherished. Even among artists, writers stand out as most likely to have their work judged artistically *and* morally. The fundamental choices we make as writers are subject to social comment and response – even to ignore a book or a writer is a kind of response.

This book

This book asks, what are the particular and specific responsibilities of a writer? It asks, to what extent are writers responsible for what they write? Is it simply that they are responsible for everything they write and for all the uses to which it might be put? Are they no more responsible than their readers? Or is it simply that they are neither more nor less responsible than when, for example, they pay their bills on time?

This book seeks to highlight some of the issues writers might ask themselves and some of the broader social or political concerns that might be taken into account when making artistic decisions. Particularly it asks: does a writer have responsibility, and if so, of what sort and to whom? What specific responsibilities arise because of the form in which a writer has chosen to work? Are these responsibilities the same for all writers, in all parts of the world, under all political and social systems? If not, why not, and how do they differ? How do the writer's chosen language and audience affect their responsibilities? What factors arise in relation to ethnicity, class, politics or sexuality? How is writing connected to issues of citizenship? What can a writer do when their sense of citizenship clashes with their sense of responsibility? How are a writer's responsibilities compromised or defined by commercial pressures, political powers or censorship, or by notions of tradition, political correctness or originality? How do writers become aware of their responsibilities, and what happens if they ignore them? This list of questions is lengthy, but doubtless a great many more will occur to the reader in the course of this book.

The first part of the book defines responsibility and looks at general issues and ideas about responsibility in writing, developing the idea that although writing is a private act it has public consequences. From this basis we can develop various perceptions or aspects of the subject, establish the scope of the topic and identify some of the issues that will be developed in Part 2.

The second part of the book offers a series of case studies, tracing in some detail the choices made by particular writers in specific contexts. The case studies pick up and develop several of the major issues identified in Part 1. They concentrate on the complex interweaving of personal, social and political issues of responsibility that fuel and affect all of those who decide to write.

Part 1

Issues

2 Tradition

This chapter examines the idea of tradition. This is not something we often think about, yet for each of us writing, language, the communities we live in, the way we do things, speech itself were all handed down to us and form part of our tradition. No matter how we might quarrel with it, we cannot ignore the fact that we and our world are products of the past. Writing, literature and literary tradition are the record of how we think about ourselves as humans: they are also the story of how we have repeatedly reinvented ourselves.

This chapter asks: What can we make of our past? In what ways does the past continue to make and use us? Does it define and limit us? Can we get away from it? Must we always speak and write the way we do? How can we break with tradition? What are our responsibilities as writers when it comes to tradition?

> This is my great-grandfather's axe. My grandfather put a new head on it and my father gave it a new handle, but this is my great-grandfather's axe.
> (Old Lithuanian saying)

Tradition, for writers, can be like this axe: practical and symbolic, meaningful and meaningless, real and fake. Always, though, it is an issue we must confront when we write, asking ourselves what responsibility we have to a tradition of writing, what responsibility we have as writers to be original, or even what responsibility we have to a tradition of originality. As with all the issues discussed in this book, every writer will have their own answers, but this chapter will highlight some of the questions that those beginning to write simply cannot avoid.

Inventing tradition

To a very great extent, to inhabit a tradition is to live in a world whose parameters were set before the lifetime of the person considering it. As historian

E. H. Carr wrote: 'History begins with the handing down of tradition; and tradition means the carrying of the habits and lessons of the past into the future' (Carr 1964: 108). But what does modern, industrialized society have in common with the more rural cultures of the past? In England, for example, much that is labelled 'traditional' – archery on the village green, morris dancers and maypoles – is extremely remote from modern daily life. Tradition, for many of us, is something linked to what has come to be called the 'heritage industry', even if we tell ourselves that in some cultures tradition still counts for more.

Another consideration is that people often appeal to the idea of tradition to imply that an age-old practice is more legitimate than a more recent habit. For example, when Prince Charles was invested as the Prince of Wales in 1969 the British establishment wanted to make claims on notions of heritage, tradition and ancient right. However, although they wanted to sanction the arrangement by appeal to tradition (the first Prince of Wales was proclaimed by Edward I in 1301), the proposed investiture ceremony in fact had no precedent, no political legitimacy in the eyes of many Welsh people and no appropriate modern ceremonial language. Palace officials decided to invent a 'traditional-sounding' ceremony using archaic language and phrases like 'liege lord', which had no modern meaning or content.

When people claim something has been done since 'time immemorial', it is certainly worth asking how far back they think 'time immemorial' stretches. Historian Eric Hobsbawm has pointed out that almost all traditions currently known to us are no more than a couple of generations old and that almost everything we now regard as traditional was 'invented' fairly recently. The 'traditional' Scottish kilt, for example, was actually invented by Thomas Rawlinson, a Lancashire cloth manufacturer, about the year 1727 (Hobsbawm and Ranger 1992: 21). Tradition may not sit easily with any precise notion of history, or any precise sequence of historical events. Those who have studied our understanding of the concept generally agree that it seems to take only two generations or a minimum of around fifty years for something to become 'traditional', and even where a particular practice has been continual, the current version may bear little resemblance to anything that went before it. For example, American tourists in Scotland have been known to complain to the Highlands and Islands Tourist Board about the dearth of thatched cottages and the prevalence of corrugated iron roofing. For most locals, though, corrugated iron is already considered a traditional building material. It has in fact only been in use since the end of World War I. Fifty years would seem to be about the minimum time needed to create a tradition.

Ambiguity is part of the concept of tradition: the idea of handing on to succeeding generations, of trading, of changing one thing into another, and of lying, all lurk behind the modern use of the word and can also be traced in the Latin root *tradere*. Cultural theorist Raymond Williams caught the twin aspects of respect for the habits of the past and the idea that the present cannot help but be a betrayal of the past when he wrote that the history of the word *tradition* 'moves again and again towards *age-old* and towards *ceremony*, *duty* and *respect*'. At the same time though, considering how little had actually been handed down to us, and how various the survivals were, each example of 'tradition' was in its own way 'both a betrayal and a surrender' (Williams 1976: 269).

Life has changed a great deal in the last fifty years and our contact with those who lived more than two lifetimes before us tends to be limited, so we might expect very few 'authentic' traditions to survive. However, Shakespeare lived seven or eight lifetimes before us and his plays are still widely performed, and the Romans, whose influence is still felt strongly in Europe, preceded us by about twenty-five lifetimes. On the one hand it is surprising that any tradition could have survived that length of time; on the other we are recognizably the same variety of humans as the earliest modern settlers who arrived in Europe about 13,000 years ago. We might be living in an age of space exploration, but much of what we are, how we think and behave, is also Stone Age. What constitutes a tradition may simply be a question of perspective.

Literary traditions

When we examine any tradition we usually see that it consists of a great many elements woven together. When the poet and critic T. S. Eliot spoke of tradition he had in mind 'the whole of the literature of Europe from Homer' and some readers now dismiss him as reactionary in response to such ideas. Yet, for all the problems inherent in Eliot's work, he is one of the very few writers to have pondered how writers fit into literary traditions, and to ask what being part of a tradition means. He insisted that tradition was really a state of mind, an awareness of what had gone before. It was not, and could not be, he said, a dogged persistence in rewriting what had been written previously, or in following forms that were already well established. For Eliot it was part of the writer's duty to be aware of, and to challenge, what had already been said and thought and felt and seen and done. It was a writer's business to find new ways of expressing new thoughts and showing new feelings. And this he saw as extending tradition:

> If the only form of tradition, of handing down, consisted in following the ways of the immediate generation before us in a blind or timid

adherence to its successes, 'tradition' should positively be discouraged. We have seen many such simple currents soon lost in the sand; and novelty is better than repetition. Tradition is a matter of much wider significance. It cannot be inherited, and if you want it you must obtain it by great labour. It involves in the first place, the historical sense, which we may call nearly indispensable to anyone who would continue to be a poet beyond his twenty-fifth year; and the historical sense involves a perception, not only of the pastness of the past, but of its presence; the historical sense compels a man to write not merely with his own generation in his bones, but with a feeling that the whole of the literature of Europe from Homer and within it the whole of the literature of his own country has a simultaneous existence and composes a simultaneous order. This historical sense [. . .] is what makes a writer traditional. And it is at the same time what makes a writer most acutely conscious of his place in time, of his own contemporaneity. No poet, no artist of any art, has his complete meaning alone. His significance, his appreciation is the appreciation of his relation to the dead poets and artists. You cannot value him alone; you must set him, for contrast and comparison, among the dead.

(Eliot 1953: 23)

Eliot also warned that tradition was not always in the current mainstream, might not be practised by the most 'significant', most popular or 'best' writers of the day, and conversely that the most distinguished literary figures were not always the bearers of the best in any tradition. In other words, traditions emerge over time and the best vantage point to view any tradition is not necessarily the present.

The literary critic F. R. Leavis, who for many people defined 'the great tradition' in English literature, referred to it as the 'picked out experience of ages regarding the finer issues of life' (Leavis and Thompson 1964: 81). For Leavis literary tradition was 'largely conveyed in language': the English language itself was a tradition for him, where words were the chief link with the past. This was not a new idea, but Leavis went beyond this to insist on the relationship between great individual literary talents and the social, cultural, political and linguistic traditions from which they spring. Considering Jane Austen, Leavis wrote that if the influences bearing on her had not 'comprised something to be called tradition' she could not have found herself as a novelist working in the English language. For Leavis her work, 'like the work of all great creative writers, gives meaning to the past' and he emphasized that traditions could emerge retrospectively with the work of an individual figure like Austen (Leavis 1948: 3).

Leavis defined the 'great tradition' of English literature as a 'seriousness

of moral purpose'. Accordingly he was not so very keen to see women writers (apart from Jane Austen and George Eliot), Irish writers, comic writers
or theatre as part of his 'great' tradition of English literature, and he even
quibbled as to whether Dickens should be included. Though he was later
to change his mind on Dickens, he found the others lacking in high moral
seriousness. But in other ways Leavis was as inclusive as the times allowed:
he included the Pole Joseph Conrad, the English outsider D. H. Lawrence
and the American Henry James. Looking back, the tradition Leavis out-
lined was of his own making and it now appears stiff and unaccommodat-
ing. Indeed, no sooner had it become enshrined in the discipline of English
Studies than it was challenged: in the 1970s in particular it was threatened
by the emergence of writing in English from Commonwealth countries,
and by the work of both American academics and a generation of working-
class graduates from the newer British universities.

The concept of tradition can be seen as a way of imposing a kind of
orthodoxy and a rigidity that discourages questioning. 'Tradition' does not
encourage us to believe that traditions change through time, but they are
undeniably fluid. This meeting of rigidity and fluidity can be particularly
difficult for writers to navigate, and the idea of a literary tradition can
prove to be one of the biggest blocks to creativity. Writers may ask themselves how they might write books as good as the ones they read, or how
fully they can emerge or depart from a tradition to become individuals
writing for themselves? If they do write something absolutely new, will anybody understand it?

Renaissance playwright Ben Jonson spoke of following the ancients 'as
guides, not commanders' and went on to explain that we have our own
experience and observations to apply to the accumulated wisdom of the
ancients (Jonson 1875). Centuries later, Irish poet W. B. Yeats wondered if
individual practitioners could ever stand out from a tradition. Surely by
doing so, he reflected, they ceased to be practitioners of that tradition. He
asked in his poem 'Among schoolchildren' how we could distinguish a tradition from what an individual practitioner made of it: 'How can we know
the dancer from the dance?' (Yeats 1973). For writers this comes down to
the question: Do I reproduce what has gone before, or do I innovate?

The tradition of decline

Eliot, and after him Leavis, spoke of a cultural decline in relation to their
ideas of tradition. Efforts such as theirs to 'uphold tradition' are often linking to the idea of preserving culture or a way of life as it existed during
some lost 'golden age', and here we encounter the long-established belief
that western culture is in decline. The idea of decline is traditional, it seems,

or we could say that 'tradition' dictates that culture is in decline. Jeremiah, preaching about 600 BC in Jerusalem, already saw in the declining standards of contemporary life a diminishing chance of bliss in the afterlife, while Alexander Pope's *Dunciad* (1728) was perhaps the first literary work in English to make clear the power of journalistic 'hacks' in shaping popular opinion through public entertainment and to see this as moral decline. The tradition continues right through to contemporary satirists' jibes at the societies in which they live. But if the idea remains that in England at least life was 'better' – more organic or wholesome – at some point in the past, when was this point?

Leavis said traditional England disappeared in the years 1907–23, but George Sturt, writing in the middle of this period, lamented that traditional England had died out by the 1890s. Thomas Hardy, writing in the 1890s, lamented that traditional England had disappeared in the 1860s. George Eliot, writing in the 1860s, lamented that traditional England had disappeared by 1830. The chain continues, all the way back to such early texts as Langland's *Piers Plowman* (1360–87), or even back to the Garden of Eden and Genesis stories of the Bible. If we are to believe our literature, history is a permanent state of decline and decline is, simply, traditional. While this is good for conservative politics and satirists, it is a little misleading when we are trying to judge the state of humanity.

A key aspect of laments about decline has been a resistance to 'mass' culture, which is characterized as encouraging mediocrity and reproduction rather than creativity, imagination or originality. The poet William Wordsworth, though he had a poor opinion of novels and journalism, made it clear in the preface to his *Lyrical Ballads* (1800) that he thought public taste had been terminally corrupted by the desire for 'outrageous stimulation'. A generation later the historian Thomas Carlyle argued that art in the future democratic world would consist only of mechanical reproduction of what had already been created. In the twentieth century we saw decline blamed on jukeboxes and transistor radios (Leavis and Leavis 1969: 5). In the 1960s radio disc jockeys were generally blamed for the decline of civilization (Hoggart 1958: 246). Anthony Burgess, in *A Clockwork Orange* (1962), had his young thugs taking drugs in a milk bar, which he saw as the real seat of corruption (Burgess 1973).

The critic Harold Bloom has argued that in American universities scholarship has been destroyed by a style of teaching he labels 'the School of Resentment', where professors of hip-hop, clones of Gallic-Germanic theory, and ideologues of gender and of various sexual persuasions attack all cultural achievement as elitist, and elevate the anti-elitist values of multiculturalism and equal opportunities in the belief that this Balkanization of literary studies celebrates the finest alternative 'the plebeian' has to offer

(Bloom 1994: 517). At best, it seems, we can do no more than aspire to classical standards and imitate 'the ancients': modernity is merely material progress.

If, as many commentators have argued, 'culture' has been busily entertaining itself to death, where does this leave writers? Radio, cinema, romantic and teenage novels and tabloid journalism have all been blamed for the decline of 'high culture'. Democracy, universal suffrage, compulsory education and mass literacy have all helped create a mass culture that is inevitably in conflict with 'high art'. So do writers have a responsibility to tradition or to the identity that goes with certain traditions? In an age dominated by Hollywood, TV commercials and soap operas, rather than the literary market for writing, is it possible to do something original? And if writers do something original, will they find a publisher or a market for their work? These are questions every writer must answer in their own way.

Tradition and society

We must remember in all of this that traditions are not global, and writers' relations to tradition are not global either. The poet and courtier Sir Philip Sidney (1554–86) noted that belonging to a writing tradition was often a function of belonging to a particular society, and that different societies displayed different views and expectations of writers:

> In Turkey, besides their law-giving divines, they have no other writers but poets. In our neighbor country Ireland, where truly learning goeth very bare, yet are their poets held in a devout reverence. Even among the most barbarous and simple Indians where no writing is, yet have they their poets who make and sing songs, which they call *areytos*, both of their ancestors' deeds and praises of their gods. [. . .] In Wales, the true remnant of the ancient Britons, as there are good authorities to show the long time they had poets, which they called bards, so through all the conquests of Romans, Saxons, Danes, and Normans, some of whom did seek to ruin all memory of learning from among them, yet do their poets even to this day last; so as it is not more notable in soon beginning than in long continuing. [. . .] Among the Romans a poet was called *vates*, which is as much as diviner, foreseer, or prophet.
>
> (Sidney 1999: 21)

Czech writer Václav Havel has been at some pains to point out that the writing traditions of east-central Europe have almost always been at variance with those of the big languages of western Europe. In east-central

Europe writers have been both more important to the preservation of cultural values and more buoyed by national culture than in western Europe. East-central Europe may have experienced a prolongation (courtesy of communism) in this respect, since communism inadvertently preserved nationalist traditions and attitudes from earlier times. But at the same time the writer from east-central Europe was also constrained by national culture. While western writers might envy colleagues in the east the degree of attention and social resonance they enjoyed, that attention and importance, that inheritance of 'national significance' assigned social roles, and in its own way bound and blocked many writers from exploring other more personal subject areas. The traditional expectation was that writers would do more than merely create readable books since they were 'the conscience of his nation'. The writers stood in for politics and politicians, they were the renewers of the national community, maintainers of the national language, awakeners of the national conscience, interpreters of the national will. All these functions, which might have been expected to lapse with the arrival of national independence, achieved a new significance under communism. In Havel's opinion, so many demands were placed on the writer that the element of responsibility became a crushing burden which helped prevent writers from addressing issues other than that of how to write under communism (Havel 1990: 72).

Breaking with tradition

At university the emphasis in literary study on the literary canon, its reinterpretation and its extension, suits academic discipline and study. But for writers, tradition and the established canon are seen in different ways. They might seem to offer the material for a productive and practical study of modes of writing to be superseded, argued with or improved upon, or in a more negative sense, they might seem to be the cause of an overwhelming sense of inadequacy and a crippling self-consciousness. But a writer's relationship with the past is not the same as an academic's relationship with the past. As the poet Adrienne Rich wrote: 'We need to know the writing of the past, and know it differently than we have ever known it; not to pass on a tradition but to break its hold over us' (Rich 1995: 465).

Creative Writing in universities, since it is as intimately bound up with the practical aspects of writing as it is with questions of where writing will go next, will inevitably address questions of tradition and the canon pragmatically, tackling them more in the nature of raw materials, ore to be mined. This is in contrast to the attitude of Literature departments where writing of the past is seen rather as a treasure hoard to be polished, revered, protected, annotated, interpreted and continually appraised.

Tradition – and literary tradition is no exception – can be made, manufactured, remade, altered and shaped at will, and as such it is useful, important, but deeply meaningless. However, we cannot easily get away from tradition since it is our language, our identity, our accumulated knowledge of the world and how to survive in it. And in writing, even the idea of a literary avant-garde breaking with tradition is something of a tradition. The dilemma for the writer comes down to one set of choices, one decision: whether we should continue the tradition of breaking with tradition, or we should break with the tradition of breaking with tradition (Boyd 1999). An absolute answer to this question can never be found, but it is crucial that writers continue to work through their relationship to their cultural past, their tradition and the issues this raises for their work, in whatever society they inhabit.

3 Power

Writers and politicians clash with remarkable ease. Indeed writing itself often seems to be antagonistic towards all varieties of politics. Yet the two professions are very closely linked. What then is the relationship between writing and politics, and what are the responsibilities of the writer towards political ideas?

This chapter asks: If writing reflects a point of view, who are the protagonists and who are the antagonists? Whose mentality is recorded by books, plays and poems? What political choices and perspectives lie behind the ways that writers perceive and represent reality? Are all writers political? Do all writers demystify politics? What political powers do writers have? Are they just part of the entertainment industry?

Literature and politics

There is still a dogged belief (perhaps hope) that somehow literature has nothing to do with politics, that serious reading and writing are a retreat from the world. Indeed, the free-wheeling personal self-expression of the 1960s created the expectation for many writers and readers that writing would be no more than a spinning out of what was inside them, rather than the writer's response to what was outside, in the world. Indeed, the professions of writer and politician are similar: both trade in visions of the future, ideologies, in influencing people; both are concerned with transmitting ideas in words. Both can sell to the public only what the public wants to buy, and both can lead the public by the nose only in the direction the public wants to go.

There have certainly been books and films where serious political debate has taken place and issues have been aired: *Lady Chatterley's Lover*, *The Female Eunuch*, *A Clockwork Orange*, *Lolita*, *Last Exit to Brooklyn*, *Natural Born Killers*, *American Psycho*. But does writing have any *real* power? This is a question writers, if they are to remain in control of what they create, must ask (and answer) every time they set out on a new piece of work. Often the debate comes down to whether writers merely reflect what they see around them and intuit changes already on the way, or whether they are, as Joseph Stalin put it, the 'engineers of human souls', people who actually help to change people.

There can be no doubt that the multivoiced post-modern world has moved a long way from the world Stalin imagined. The rise of Hollywood, the ubiquity of TV, the power of advertising, the common denominator of the 'the soaps', the advent of the global economy, the Internet, chat rooms, telephone sex, and almost instant TV news reporting from around the globe, all mean that the babble of voices has increased massively and governments have to work very hard indeed to keep anything hidden from the public gaze. The critic Alvarez wrote:

> We no longer have local wars, we have world wars, which involve the civilians quite as deeply as the military. Where once, at worst, regiments of professional soldiers were wiped out, now whole cities go. Instead of individual torture and sadism, we have concentration camps run scientifically as death factories. The disintegration, to put it mildly, has reached proportions which make it increasingly difficult to ignore. Once upon a time, the English could safely believe that Evil was something that happened on the Continent, or farther off, in the Empire where soldiers were paid to take care of it. To believe this now requires at best an extraordinary single-mindedness, at worst stupidity.
>
> (Alvarez 1971: 21)

Hegemony

Writing has had some effect on the world. Alexander Solzhenitsyn's *One Day in the Life of Ivan Denisovitch* (1962) helped put an end to the Gulag; Upton Sinclair's *The Jungle* (1906) helped to expose the Chicago slaughterhouses and bring about a change in the law; Joseph Heller's *Catch 22* (1961) fed into the backlash against the Vietnam war; and Salman Rushdie's *The Satanic Verses* (1988) helped focus western attention on the rise of Islamic fundamentalism. However, in terms of *power* to effect change and alter the world, for writers this simply does not exist. Very few artists have physical or political power.

Power is no longer simply a gunboat commodity in the sense it was in the nineteenth-century European empires. Political power is no longer simply an asymmetric relationship of ruler and ruled. It is neither here nor there. It is increasingly diffuse, personal, social, cultural; it is amorphous, exercised and reciprocated by myriad threads of influence and contact. Power and its opposite operate as ideology, world view or collective activity: it may consist simply of humans working together or it may be character-ized as massive economic blackmail. What little power literature has is exercised not through force and coercion, but through the market, through culture, through questioning, affecting the way people think and feel, by saying things that have not been said before, by dragging to light emotions and reactions that were previously invisible, and by plugging into or expressing what is merging. Writing works not through the direct exercise of political power, but through discussion, discrimination and dissemina-tion of values. As the Polish poet Zbigniew Herbert put it, for him political opposition to communism came down to taste:

> It didn't require great character at all
> our refusal disagreement and resistance
> we had a shred of necessary courage
> but fundamentally it was a matter of taste
> Yes taste
>
> (Herbert 1985: 69)

Herbert, though he does not say it, is talking about *hegemony*.

The word *hegemony* was borrowed from the Greek *hegemonia*, meaning authority. In the nineteenth century this word was used to describe the dominance of one state power over another, but since that time the word has been refined, mainly by the Italian revolutionary Antonio Gramsci (1891–1937). Gramsci claimed that there was more to power than power itself, that direct political power, control of the armed forces, the power of coercion, was never the full picture. He taught that political and cultural domination operate under state power, but only with consent. He said that political domination could only succeed in the long term by gaining and holding consent. Governments could only hope to stay in office if they gained and retained the consent of the populace. In the long run, he insisted, consent was far more important than force: a shared world vision and agreement as to the processes at work in the world were more impor-tant to maintaining a leading position in society. In his *Prison Notebooks* Gramsci warned that a party, even if it achieved political dominance, still had to be seen to offer intellectual and moral leadership. Gramsci's point was that the dominant ideology is always reflected in the structure, consciousness and daily culture of social and political institutions, but that these were not immutable. He argued that leadership, particularly in a democracy, is won by appearing to be more wise, more able, more morally in touch with the populace than any alternative. Hegemony seeks not subjects and slaves, but willing converts, enthusiastic followers and 'lieutenants' (Gramsci 1973: 57).

The critic Raymond Williams considered that hegemony was 'especially important in societies in which electoral politics and public opinion were significant factors, and in which social practice was seen to depend on consent to certain dominant ideas which in fact expressed the needs of the dominant class' (Williams 1976: 118). Williams was aware that writing was fragmentary and self-contradictory, that it was part of the questioning that allowed change rather than a vision to which society aspired. Hegemony sees the maintenance of the ruling system as its end, sees a commonality of interests, creates a common way of seeing the world, a way of deciding what is 'normal', offers a shared sense of what is 'real' and what is 'common-sense'. Gramsci and Williams recognized that intellectual arguments, while they may form quite quickly, take a long time to operate and that intellectuals (particularly writers) are involved in a very long-term project to influence society by opening it up to the possibility of change, while society and its institutions seek to influence writers to support the status quo.

Nobel Prize winner Wole Soyinka, picking up on this point, has lamented the scale of the writers' failure to alert the world to the reality of post-colonial African life:

> The African writer has done nothing to vindicate his existence, nothing to indicate that he is even aware that this awful collapse has taken place. For he has generally been without vision. [. . .] Reality, the ever-present fertile reality, was ignored by the writer and resigned to the new visionary – the politician. [. . .] The average published writer in the first few years of the post-colonial era was the most celebrated skin of inconsequence to obscure the true flesh of the African dilemma. [. . .] In the movement towards chaos in modern Africa, the writer did not anticipate. The understanding language of the outside world, 'birth pains', the near-fatal euphemism for death throes, absolved him from responsibility. He was content to turn his eye backwards in time and prospect in archaic fields for forgotten gems which would dazzle and distract the present. But never inwards, never, truly into the present, never into the obvious symptoms of the niggling, warning, predictable present, from which alone lay the salvation of ideals.
>
> (Soyinka 1998: 17)

When the western powers realized (somewhere between the end of World War II and the end of the Vietnam war) that invasion was too costly to be an effective way of maintaining control of territory, the concept of hegemony made it clear that the west could maintain its power by providing the world with a major cultural input in terms of political ideas, the financial culture that went with the English language, through creating wants the world did not know it had, and by providing ways in which these wants could be satisfied. That is, by drawing the rest of the world into the way the west lived. The desire to 'own' a motor car, TV, video, CD, DVD, designer running shoes or a mobile phone, eat hamburgers, drink Coca Cola and wear a Benetton sweater, etc. is now nearly universal. We can safely assume that if people do not want these things it is probably because they live without electricity in some obscure corner of the world and have simply not heard about them. This economic and cultural strategy, backed up where necessary by military might, has generally been more effective and financially rewarding than invasion.

On the other hand, much of the Muslim world is now struggling with the hegemony of the west and the economic power of capitalism. Islamic fundamentalism is not purely religious: it is opposed to much of the way the west lives, does not see the world as a chaos of opportunism where the individual must make his own way at any price, and resists western emphasis upon the individual as consumer. For all its problems, the Islamic world does not see every Third World peasant as a potential consumer struggling to get to McDonald's.

Writing as demystification

Novelist and essayist George Orwell asked whether every writer was political. His answer was:

> There is no such thing as genuinely nonpolitical literature, and least of all in an age like our own, when fears, hatreds, and loyalties of a directly political kind are near to the surface of everyone's consciousness. Even a single taboo can have an all-round crippling effect upon the mind, because there is always the danger that any thought which is freely followed up may lead to the forbidden thought.
>
> (Orwell 1986a: 81)

Václav Havel said writing for the theatre was a highly political act. He did not mean this in a party-political sense, but in the broadest and most serious sense:

> In other words in no way as an instrument of propaganda for this or that political ideology, conception, power, part or group but as something which has the innate characteristic that it is not indifferent to the

fate of the human *polis*, that it has a live, penetrative relationship with the social reality of its country and its time and that it attains its 'timeless' and 'universal' understanding through its concrete knowledge of its place and its time, being firmly created, on which to a certain extent it is dependent, and to which it is bound for its very existence. The theatre is not therefore political according to the political power to which it bows or the politics which it proclaims, but according to how deeply it mirrors and reflects the social happenings of its time, and raises, formulates and demonstrates the social problems of its contemporaries and is able to observe its themes through the prism of the sensibility of its age.

(Havel 1967: 879)

For him the main task of writing is to demystify the workings – hegemony – of the state. And this can be done in various ways, by emphasizing different things, but mainly by insisting that writing is not simply a matter of providing material for the entertainment and advertising industries, nor even about producing satire. Writers are not the sole bearers of truth. They are only a tiny part of a much larger picture and a much larger struggle. Writing, they insist, can be restorative of knowledge, consciousness and awareness. This may be so, but it is a situation full of baffling paradoxes.

The paradoxes

The arts, publishing, state patronage, theatres, libraries, schools and universities in both the USA and the UK may be staffed, financed and managed by radical, aware, sensitive professionals, yet by and large both states remain sluggish and reactionary with regard to the arts, preferring established, historically legitimated art forms, reflecting conservative values rather than the avant-garde values of many arts practitioners. Even in the liberal democracies of western Europe, writing and publishing may be subsidized (minimally) by the state, but if so it is by a civil service which is generally opposed to other sexualities, nationalities, languages, identities, religions and skin colours, and where institutions resist the very idea that these things are in any way connected to the arts.

Writing reflects the whole life of a society, not a slice of that life or a perspective on it. Inclusions and exclusions from that vision tell us something about the structure of that life. Writing cannot escape the conflicts of gender, sexuality, language, nationality and identity any more than it can escape the conflict between the classes. All artistic endeavours are historically conditioned through the structure of society. Writing reflects social, economic and political forces through artistic forms and conventions in the marketplace. In the UK, for example, the fact that plays like *No Sex Please, We're British, Boeing Boeing* and *The Mousetrap* dominated London theatres for over thirty years (before being overtaken by musicals like *Cats*) reflects very accurately a historical response to very particular social, cultural and political pressures.

From time to time writers may think they are exercising considerable influence over events, when in fact the very opposite is true. An example is the British alternative theatre movement of the 1970s which sprang up partly as a response to the conservatism of the London West End theatre scene. This movement, which helped launch the careers of distinguished playwrights like John Arden, Trevor Griffiths, Caryl Churchill, David Hare, Howard Brenton, David Edgar, David Mercer, Edward Bond and John McGrath, many of whom are now regarded as modern classics, believed itself to be very successful in propagandizing for the liberal left. However, it was Mike Leigh's TV play *Abigail's Party* (1977) that provided the more accurate insight into what lay in store. Leigh, without any open discussion of politics, laid bare the spiteful reactionary ambition of the British middle class and the discontent that would in 1979 elect and maintain the Conservative Party in power for nearly eighteen years. It is perhaps not surprising that 'alternative theatre' was one of the first victims of this new government's 'good housekeeping' policy.

Awards and prizes

A literary prize is always a good thing for a writer to receive: the money and the publicity that accompany such recognition can help a writer enormously. We must be careful to distinguish between a literary award – where the judges are usually other writers – and state honours awarded for political reasons. A literary award is significantly different from an award offered by politicians, governments or the state. However, in each case the writer has to ask the questions: What kind of award is it, and does the acceptance of this award contradict the writer's principles and responsibilities in any way?

For example, in the UK in November 2003 the novelist Hari Kunzru refused to accept the distinguished *Mail on Sunday* John Llewellyn Rhys Prize for fiction. Kunzru said:

> The *Mail*'s campaign to persuade its readers that they live in dangerous times, that the white cliffs of Dover are about to be 'swamped' or 'overrun' by swan-eating Kosovans or HIV positive central Africans would, in isolation, be merely amusing. However, the attitudes it promotes towards immigrants have real consequences. Bricks through windows.

Knives in guts. [. . .] I want my work to help reduce prejudice, not reinforce it.

(Kunzru 2003)

A few days later the poet Benjamin Zephaniah revealed that he had just turned down the offer of an OBE (Order of the British Empire) from Buckingham Palace:

Me? I thought, OBE me? Up yours, I thought. I get angry when I hear that word 'empire'; it reminds me of slavery, it reminds me of thousands of years of brutality, it reminds me of how my foremothers were raped and my forefathers brutalised. [. . .] I am profoundly anti-empire.

(Zephaniah 2003)

And just a few days later a civil servant revealed, in a leak to *The Times*, that in the last twenty years more than 300 people had turned down honours ranging from an OBE to a Companion of Honour and even a Life Peerage. Many of those who turned down awards from Buckingham Palace were respected writers, including: J. G. Ballard, Michael Frayn, David Bowie, Alan Bennett, John Cleese, Roald Dahl, George Melly, Robert Graves, Graham Greene, Doris Lessing, Aldous Huxley, V. S. Naipaul and Evelyn Waugh. John Le Carré, Philip Larkin and J. B. Priestley are also thought to have turned down honours. Some who decided not to accept honours from the Queen said they felt that as the award had been suggested by the Prime Minister it was 'political' and therefore inappropriate. Some refused all connection to an award by royalty; others said that the Empire was outdated, retrograde and patronizing. Several clearly objected to the hierarchy of the awards system, and while Graham Greene, V. S. Naipaul and Doris Lessing turned down minor awards, they did not refuse higher-ranking awards offered to them later (Alibhai-Brown 2003). J. G. Ballard wrote:

I might have been tempted to call myself Commander Ballard – it has a certain ring. I could see a yachting cap and rum ration as perks of the job. If I was French and was awarded the legion of honour, I might well accept. But as a republican, I can't accept an honour awarded by the monarch. There's all that bowing and scraping and mummery at the palace. It's the whole climate of deference to the monarch and everything else it represents. They just seem to perpetuate the image of Britain as too much pomp and not enough circumstance. It's a huge pantomime where tinsel takes the place of substance.

A lot of these medals are orders of the British Empire, which is a bit ludicrous. The dreams of empire were only swept away relatively recently, in the '60s. [. . .] It goes with the whole system of hereditary privilege and rank, which should be swept away. It uses snobbery and social self consciousness to guarantee the loyalty of large numbers of citizens who should feel their loyalty is to fellow citizens and the nation as a whole. We are a deeply class-divided society.

I think it is deplorable when left-wing playwrights like David Hare, who have worn their socialist colours on both sleeves for so many years, should accept a knighthood. God almighty the man actually knelt down in front of the Queen.

(Ballard 2003)

Perhaps the most famous example of a writer making a political point about a literary award is John Berger. In spite of the hostility of the critics and reviewers, his novel *G* won *The Guardian* Fiction Prize and the James Tait Black Memorial Prize. In November 1972 it was awarded the Booker Prize for Fiction, worth £5,000 to the winner – serious money for any writer in those days. However, in his acceptance speech at the award dinner Berger upset the US industrial giants Booker-McConnell, the British literary scene and the press on both sides of the Atlantic. He said:

One does not have to be a novelist seeking very subtle connections to trace the five thousand pounds of this prize back to the economic activities from which they came, Booker McConnell have had extensive trading interests in the Caribbean for over 130 years. The modern poverty of the Caribbean is the direct result of this and similar exploitation. One of the consequences of this Caribbean poverty is that hundreds of thousands of West Indians have been forced to come to Britain as migrant workers. Thus my book about migrant workers would be financed from the profits made directly out of them or their relatives and ancestors.

More than that, however, is involved. The industrial revolution, and the inventions and culture which accompanied it and which created modern Europe, was initially financed by profits from the slave trade. And the fundamental nature of relationship between Europe and the rest of the world, between black and white, has not changed. In *G* the statue of the four chained Moors is the most important single image of the book. This is why I have to turn this prize against itself. And I propose to do so by sharing it in a particular way. The half I give away will change the half I keep.

First let me make the logic of my position really clear. It is not a question of guilt or bad conscience. It certainly is not a question of philanthropy. It is not even, first and foremost, a question of politics. It is a question of my continuing development as a writer: the issue is between me and the culture which has formed me.

Before the slave trade began, before the European de-humanised himself, before he clenched himself on his own violence there must have been a moment when black and white approached each other with the amazement of potential equals. The moment passed. And henceforth the world was divided between potential slaves and potential slave masters. And the European carried this mentality back to his own society. It became part of his way of seeing everything.

The novelist is concerned with the interaction between individual and historical destiny. The historical destiny of our time is becoming clear. The oppressed are breaking through the wall of silence which was built into their minds by their oppressors. And in their struggle against exploitation and neo-colonialism – but only through and by virtue of this common struggle – it is possible for the descendants of the slave and the slave master to approach each other again with the amazed hope of potential equals.

This is why I intend to share the prize with those West Indians in and from the Caribbean who are fighting to put an end to their exploitation. The London-based Black Panther movement has arisen out of the bones of what Bookers and other companies have created in the Caribbean; I want to share this prize with the Black Panther movement because they resist both as black people and workers the further exploitation of the oppressed. And because, through their Black People's Information Centre, they have links with the struggle in Guyana, the seat of Booker McConnell's wealth, in Trinidad and throughout the Caribbean: the struggle whose aim is to expropriate all such enterprises.

(Dyer 1986: 92)

Berger's actions made him extremely unpopular with the US and UK establishments, but his conviction that it was right for him to do this was strong. Criticism did not stop him doing exactly what he said he would. Nor did it stop him as a writer from pursuing these themes further. We can see in his speech the differences between the kind of power writers wield and the kind of power big business and politicians wield. We can also see very clearly his personal struggle with the legacy of historical events and the long-term siege for moral influence that concerned Gramsci.

4   Accuracy

This chapter looks at some of the different kinds of inaccuracy and explores the social, political and historical context in which these can become problematic.

At its simplest, accuracy is a matter of getting facts right. For example, it is not unknown for even the most successful of sci-fi writers to have the earth revolve in the wrong direction. However, facts are rarely simple, and interpretation of facts is never straightforward. At its most trivial, soap opera characters merely get tangled up in their script. But at its worst an inaccuracy can rewrite history and may be seriously offensive.

The crucial factor for writers – the thing that decides whether it is important or not – is the context in which the inaccuracy takes place. This chapter asks: What are the writer's responsibilities when it comes to matters of fact?

Sir,
In your otherwise beautiful poem (The Vision of Sin) there is a verse which reads:

> Every moment dies a man,
> Every moment one is born.

Obviously, this cannot be true and I suggest that in the next edition you have it read:

> Every moment dies a man,
> Every moment 1 1/16 is born.

Even this is slightly in error but should be sufficiently accurate for poetry.

(Charles Babbage, letter to Lord Tennyson)

Accuracy and the soaps

In the US soap *Dallas*, viewing figures plummeted after Bobby Ewing was shot and killed at the end of series six. In desperation the directors decided to bring Bobby back in series eight. The intervening series seven was explained away as a bad dream by Pam, Bobby's wife. However, the script-writers were left with a series of inconsistencies: actors had changed, sets had been destroyed. Viewers of series eight noticed that characters that had been part of Pam's dream were still present, and others who had been there before the dream, had disappeared. The house that Ray and Donna lost in the floods during Pam's dream, was not reinstated.

In 2000 the press was much exercised by an inconsistency in the sitcom *Friends*. The character Ross, had for years maintained that he lost his virginity with his wife, Carol. Now he claimed he lost his virginity with a cleaner at university. Perhaps Ross had realized that what he thought was sex, was not. Perhaps what had taken place between him and the cleaner was, well, something else? Perhaps the experience with the cleaner was so awful he had blotted it from his memory. There was a similar moment in the sitcom *Cheers* and its spin-off *Frasier*. In *Cheers* Frasier Crane was known to be an orphan. However, when he moved to Seattle to star in his own show, his father suddenly materialized. Was this a bout of amnesia or poor scriptwriting? Or were more laughs to be had with a new situation?

It has always been difficult to keep track of characters in the soaps. In the early 1960s in the UK soap *Coronation Street*, Elsie Tanner's lodger went out to buy a pint of milk and never came back. He didn't go missing, there was no police inquiry. The scriptwriters simply forgot about him. The next time the actor who had played the lodger appeared on TV he was lead singer in a successful band called Herman's Hermits; his fame as a pop star and several hit records made it impossible for him to return, with or without the milk.

In the highly successful UK soap *EastEnders*, Frank Butcher's decision to leave his wife demanded a complete loss of memory and his absence for more than a year. When he returned it was to find a new wife. And when his character began to run out of steam, it was merely a matter of convenience to have him suddenly develop an aversion to his new wife and a suicidal passion for his ex-wife. When his ex-wife's new husband found out that she had been having an affair with her ex-husband he threw her out of the house. Almost immediately the BBC switchboard was jammed as hundreds of people rang up to say that it was in fact *her* house. The scriptwriters apologized.

History and Hollywood

Films are particularly liable to scrutiny. Hollywood's 'mistakes' can be the result of simple error or the result of the casual handling of actuality. *Robin Hood: Prince of Thieves* (1993) is an example of Hollywood making what it likes of reality. At the start of the film Robin escapes from a jail in the Middle East and, accompanied by a Moorish warrior, makes his way to England. He arrives at the white cliffs of Dover, and says: 'By nightfall we will celebrate with my father.' His father's castle is in Nottingham. Even with a fast car and a motorway it is a journey of several hours. On horseback it would have taken several days. Robin and his companion are on foot. In the next scene we see them on Hadrian's wall, a long way north of their destination. The Muslim warrior wants to pray, and lacking sight of the sun (this part is accurate) asks Robin which way is east. Robin, claiming he is on his own land now, only a few miles from home, cheerfully points south. For Hollywood, Dover, Nottingham and Hadrian's wall are nothing more than bits of curious bric-a-brac which help make Britain a lure for tourists. The direction of Mecca, like the geography of Britain, is not important.

Saving Private Ryan (1998) is probably the most grimly realistic war film ever made, yet it upset D-Day veterans because, with a few slighting words, it dismissed the struggles of the British, Canadian and Polish Armies to win a strategic advantage for US forces. The implication of the film is that the US was the only real Allied presence in Normandy. The film set incredibly high standards of realization and effects. But that realism is itself a problem. The film follows a squad of Rangers who land on Omaha Beach and three days later are sent inland to search for Private Ryan. Eventually they pass through a glider landing zone where a pilot explains how his glider came to crash. Without telling the pilot somebody had put a steel plate into the floor of the glider to protect a three-star general. The effect was to alter the trim characteristics of the glider making it almost impossible to land safely. The pilot shows a general's body and jeep still stuck in the wreckage, commenting ruefully that twenty-two men died 'all on account of one man'. Clearly this reflects the main theme and title of the film. But there is an odd inaccuracy.

The glider shown is the CG4A Waco. It had a flight crew of two and a payload of 3,750 lb, that is *either* thirteen to fifteen infantrymen, *or* a jeep, a small towed gun and a gun crew of four. We know the glider in the film was carrying a jeep because we see it in the wreckage. We are not shown a towed gun. But even if the glider was not carrying a gun, it was not capable of carrying the jeep and twenty-three men. So what happened? Did Spielberg's scriptwriters just get it wrong? Is the pilot hiding something? Was there an incident we have not been told about?

The question of how many men a glider could carry is probably important only to military historians: it does not concern those who just want to be entertained. Nor does it alter the moral of the story. Or does it? In almost every other aspect – weaponry, tactics and injuries – the film is incredibly detailed and realistic. So why fault it on such a small thing? This tiny lapse is important because it is part of a much wider picture. The director's intention is clearly that this should not be dismissed as 'just a film'. The film tells the story of a group of men giving their lives to save another man, trying to find one decent thing in a war which they feel has made them do and see indecent things. The film picks up important themes from Spielberg's earlier *Schindler's List* (1993), where it is said of Oscar Schindler that he who saves a life saves a world entire.

Between *Schindler's List* and *Saving Private Ryan* Spielberg had also been involved in another project called *The Last Days*, an oral testimony of Holocaust survivors. Spielberg was also involved in making a TV mini series called *Band of Brothers* which followed the story of a group of soldiers from the 506 US Airborne Regiment through World War II from D-Day to the capture of Berchtesgaden. That it was based on a carefully researched book by an established historian who had followed the fortunes of one particular group of men meant little to those who felt that in *Saving Private Ryan* and in *Band of Brothers* the USA had been seen to win the war in Europe without Allied help. That these films should be linked in viewers' minds was intentional. That they were Spielberg's idea of the reality of the event was undeniable. But in this context, was the glider a mistake or an emotional manipulation important to the main theme of the film? If it is not a mistake then it is an emotional manipulation.

Concerns over accuracy drove the director of the film *U-571* (2000) to surround himself with ex-submariners to give technical advice. Yet the film had a US ship seizing an important Enigma code machine where in fact a British ship had done this. It also had the USA at war with Germany at a time when the USA had not yet entered the war. It had German fighter planes flying over the mid-Atlantic, and German destroyers in the same area, when in fact they both lacked the range to get there. Protests at this film's rewriting of history drove the British Prime Minister to address Parliament on the subject.

The subtext of protest at *U-571* was that, as in *Saving Private Ryan*, the US 'effort' had been given massive coverage to the detriment of everyone else. On the other hand, throughout the late 1940s and 1950s Britain made a great many films about World War II in which the US contribution appeared to be negligible. The Americans did not complain, possibly because Hollywood too had started rewriting World War II even before it ended. The film *Objective Burma!* (1944) managed to suggest that the US won the Burma campaign. The release of this film in the UK caused a full-scale diplomatic incident and it was subsequently banned until 1952 (Milne 1989).

The context of these things is important. It is possible that being written out of World War II is the price the British pay for having any film industry at all. In the year 2000 US film makers spent over £750,000,000 in British studios. The ten episodes of *Band of Brothers* took nine months to film in Hertfordshire, employed 500 speaking actors and 10,000 extras. Catering on the set ran to 600–800 meals per day and the production had a total budget of £83,000,000, of which 70 per cent went to British employees (Gritten 2001: 42). The award of a knighthood to Steven Spielberg in the 2001 New Year Honours list recognized his talent as a film maker, his importance to British film making and his importance to the finance that underpins what is left of the British film industry. Without US investment and spending power the British film industry would not have been able to make films like *Billy Elliot*, *The Full Monty*, *Four Weddings and a Funeral*, *Notting Hill*, *East is East* and *Bridget Jones's Diary* (Smith 2001: 16).

Worries about the power of Hollywood to re-create and rewrite history were further compounded on the release of the $135,000,000 Disney blockbuster *Pearl Harbor* (2001). In that film much was made of the sneakiness of the 1941 Japanese attack, which dragged the USA into World War II. However, there was no attempt to make it clear that the Japanese were already at war with the British, French, Dutch and Chinese. Much was made of the slaughter, but there was no mention of Japanese-American or Hawaiian casualties. Nor was there any indication of the anti-Japanese hysteria that followed the attack in which over 110,000 Japanese-Americans were dispossessed and interned. Nor was mention made of the thousands of Japanese-Americans who volunteered for military service as a result of the attack.

Anti-Japanese feeling has been a legacy of considerable difficulty for the USA. P. K. Dick made great play of this in his 1962 novel *The Man in the High Castle* (Dick 1987). In 1988 President Ronald Reagan gave $20,000 and an official apology to each and every Japanese-American who had been interned during the war. But in 1991, on the anniversary of the attack, Japanese-American owned buildings and businesses in Los Angeles were attacked by gangs seeking revenge for the events of 1941. It was feared that *Pearl Harbor*, released on the 60th anniversary of the attack and during a long drawn out trade-war between Japan and the USA, increased Japanese tension about the US troops still stationed in Japan, stirred anti-Japanese feeling and once again characterized the Japanese as the enemy.

For Hollywood these may be fine stories. But clearly there is an element of adapting history to the screen which simplifies and rewrites events – and not always for purely cinematic reasons. For those who took part in the war and for the families of those who did not return, however, these are not events to be altered at will. There are people still alive who took part in D-Day, in the Battle of the Atlantic and in the Burma campaign, and many more who lost loved ones. Often it is what lies behind inaccuracy, rather than the inaccuracy itself, that gives offence. Inaccuracy often indicates something is adrift, that the film makers are 'twisting things' to make a point that perhaps has little to do with the original event. The worry is that film-goers take these films as the truth and assume that the USA beat the Nazis and the Japanese single-handed.

The other concern is that in a context of growing right-wing activity, neo-Nazis and Holocaust deniers can make use of any and every slip or invention to bolster their cause and foster their own rewriting of history. Inaccuracies in films about the Holocaust certainly aid them in dividing communities and promoting racism.

Accuracy and 'serious' writing

Louis de Bernieres's *Captain Corelli's Mandolin* (1994), set on the Greek island of Cephalonia, has been the subject of increasingly bitter criticism. De Bernieres, it seems, came out in favour of the murderous prewar Greek dictatorship led by Metaxas and misrepresented the communist wartime resistance movement by showing them as blood thirsty brigands, keener on the rape and torture of fellow Greeks than on fighting the Nazis. De Bernieres was at first welcomed to Cephalonia and praised by the mayor for attracting pleasant tourists who came book in hand. Now de Bernieres is reluctant to return to the island. With the translation of the book into Greek and the appearance of the film, he reluctantly admitted he might have 'got it wrong'. However, the film scriptwriter, Shawn Slovo, said that he found the book 'offensive and inaccurate'. Although the Greeks have taken a dislike to the book, they have seen only parts of it, since de Bernieres was persuaded to remove the most offensive passages from the Greek translation before it was published (Milne 2001: 19).

In TV war reporting, as demonstrated by the Falklands War, in both Gulf Wars and in the Balkan Wars, accuracy has become increasingly problematic. In 1999, for example, Ron Redmond, spokesman for the United Nations High Commision for Refugees, announced at a press conference detailed reports of mass rape, slaughter, torture and the abuse of corpses in three villages in the Lipljan area of Kosovo. He spoke as if this was a huge event with hundreds of people involved. Later, when pressed by journalist Audrey Gillan for figures, Redmond admitted he had heard from refugees of five or six incidents of rape, but had no names or witnesses and had no way of verifying the story he was telling. A short while later Gillan heard a reporter repeat Redmond's story on BBC TV. Later Robin Cook, British Foreign Secretary, took up the story and spoke of a special rape camp set up by the Serbs, to which women, sifted from the refugee columns, were taken 'and forced to undergo systematic rape'. He claimed to have evidence 'from many refugees'. And yet among the refugees interviewed by the officers of the Organization for Security and Co-operation in Europe, and by Human Rights Watch, both of which were compiling evidence against the Serbs for the International War Crimes Tribunal in The Hague, though several spoke of rape, no one spoke of a special 'rape camp'.

It has been suggested that the story was initiated by the Kosovo Liberation Army, who were desperate to get NATO to send troops into the area. There is no suggestion that Serbian forces did not behave badly, that rape and massacre did not take place. But it is clear the figure of 100,000 Albanian dead has now been whittled down to about 3,000. Gillan has said this verifying of 'facts' was a lesson in how propaganda works in a modern war (Gillan 2000: 20).

That stories become exaggerated in war is perhaps inevitable. That such stories should also become propaganda material is also inevitable. However, arguments about accuracy are not just about what constitutes a fact. They are about the selection of facts, the context in which facts are seen, how facts are to be interpreted. To be taken in by the propaganda of hate makes us all feel foolish, suspicious and dirty: now we feel we have to mistrust what appear to be eyewitness accounts. Next time we suspect we are being fed a line by the military or by politicians – perhaps next time we are told that a country has Weapons of Mass Destruction – we will be less inclined to believe. But next time it may be for real. How will we know?

In dealing with fiction, the soaps and Hollywood a healthy scepticism has always been essential: the organizations that propagate them have agendas of their own and these do not necessarily include telling the truth. There is accuracy and there is artistic licence, just as there is History and there is Hollywood. It is increasingly difficult, and increasingly important, to distinguish between them. To be paranoid about these things is not to be wrong. A paranoid is, after all, someone who has just found out what is really going on.

5 Kitsch

We live at a time of unprecedented mass consumption and increasing homogeneity of markets. Literature and writing are part of this: publishing is a business and publishers aim to promote books that appeal to the widest possible range of readers.

Originality and kitsch, its opposite, are the subject of this next chapter. Kitsch is a concept that helps us understand the artistic and creative environment, in which writers and artists of all kinds operate and the difficulties they face in trying to create and sell new work.

This chapter asks: To what extent can contemporary writers be authentic or original? If a writer happens to write something authentic and original, will it get published? Should writers try to be authentic and original, or should they just find new ways to recycle the successes of the past?

Kitsch and originality

It is difficult to speak of originality or authenticity in writing without first speaking of their opposite – kitsch.

The word kitsch comes from German: *verkitschen* means to make cheap or cheapen, and *kitschen* means to collect trash. Kitsch is defined in the *Oxford English Dictionary* as: decoration characterized by worthless pretension to art: poor, trashy, slapdash taste, something cobbled together; to render worthless; to affect with sentimentality and vulgarity.

The German novelist Hermann Broch (1886–1951) emphasized that kitsch was not merely a matter of degeneracy or ill-will, but a matter of taste. Broch included in his definition of kitsch all artists pursuing 'beauty' as a literary category, along with all those who tried to make a closed system of art, cutting it off from outside considerations, usually with the phrase 'Art for art's sake'. For Broch the real problems lay in the seductiveness and apparent normality of kitsch, the ubiquity of cliché and the commercial temptation of unchallenging literary production.

The German novelist Thomas Mann (1875–1955) also saw populist literature and mass taste as a kind of wretchedness, 'the murder of mind and spirit' which pandered to narrow imaginations and limited abilities. He felt that serious writing was often 'unsuited to the masses' and he was in favour of 'audacious, unrestrained advance and research' in writing (Mann 1968: 311).

The first use of kitsch in English is recorded in the OED as 1926. However the word became a fully functioning part of the English language only in the 1980s, when Czech novelist Milan Kundera brought the word into focus. He made explicit links between kitsch, writing and politics:

> The feeling induced by kitsch must be a kind the multitudes can share. Kitsch may not, therefore, depend on an unusual situation; it must derive from the basic images people have engraved in their memories: the ungrateful daughter, the neglected father, children running on the grass, the motherland betrayed, first love. Kitsch causes two tears to flow in quick succession. The first tear says: How nice to see children running on the grass! The second tear says: How nice to be moved, together with all mankind, by children running on the grass! It is the second tear that makes kitsch kitsch. The brotherhood of man on earth will be possible only on a base of kitsch. And no one knows this better than politicians. Whenever a camera is in the offing, they immediately run to the nearest child, lift it in the air, kiss it on the cheek. Kitsch is the aesthetic ideal of all politicians and all political Movements.
>
> (Kundera 1984a: 250)

Kundera considered kitsch to mean 'absolute artistic opportunism capable of drawing on anything in order to move people emotionally [. . .] eclecticism with one imperative: that it must please'. He linked this to the sense that for him political parties and elections were unthinkable without kitsch. Kitsch, he insisted, was inevitable. 'The function of the successful politician is to please. He is meant to please the largest number of people humanly possible, and to please so many you must rely on the clichés they want to hear' (Kundera 1984b: 29). In effect Kundera said, we live in a world of artistic and political kitsch, of democratic commercial totalitarianism.

Originality and mass media

Kitsch means that artistic worth is a social given, dictated by the 'popular' mass market, imposed by business, enforced by the promise of 'success' and the threat of 'failure'. Kitsch is the aesthetic that says there is no such thing as society, there is only the individual; millions of 'individuals' all saying: 'Me, me, me: I'm different.' Kitsch is now transient, low cost, mass produced, big business, obsessed with fame, sex, glamour, boredom, stimulation and image. It now has a flippant exuberance that lends itself to self-parody, recycling and an endless obsession with the world of TV, pop music and fashion. Those involved in the production of kitsch both mean and do not mean what they say, have a belief in, and simultaneously no belief in, what they are doing. They are serious and ironic. They look to historical forms, not to innovate but to parody. Compared to this, serious artists of all kinds seem old fashioned and definitely out of date.

Kitsch wallows in surrender, in giving up the attempt to discriminate, to affect the world, to exercise aesthetic judgement, to be independent. It is a kind of lowest common denominator, sanctioned now by the fragmented and relativist judgements of post-modernism, and by the commercial judgement of the marketplace, where everything (artistic work, even democracy itself) is reduced to its money value, its sale price. It is easy to give examples of non-literary kitsch: a chimps' tea party, an expensive silk carpet woven with Princess Diana's face, mugs and tea-towels of British Royal Weddings, 1970s Hooked on Classics albums, porcelain figures of children with sheep or dogs or birds, carved wooden hedgehogs, glass paperweights with snow scenes, almost everything associated with 'the season of goodwill', Country and Western albums featuring songs about blind boys and dogs, Dolly Parton, the Carpenters.

Kitsch, like post-modern literary theory, really sees very little difference between a bus ticket and Joyce's *Ulysses*, between the death camps and a 1960s Country and Western album, between genocide and Chopin, though it does have its preferences. Contemporary kitsch has been clearly connected to politics and ethics and is apparent in the character of the murderous psychopath, Patrick Bateman, in Bret Easton Ellis's *American Psycho* (1991).

Is kitsch just mass production?

Clearly kitsch need not be tied to a repressive political regime: it is commercial, economic and democratic. Kitsch sees itself as personal, exclusive, mine, not available to everyone. However, in reality it is general, available to all, neither exclusive nor personal. The key factor is that it is sanctioned by the judgement of the marketplace, where everything (artistic work, democracy) is reduced to its commercial value.

What kitsch does is to take an authentic and original artistic revelation and turn it into a cliché, a formula, a standard way of showing and seeing. We can see this blurring of judgement in the way TV soaps recycle ideas, plots, characters, in the way that soaps are followed so avidly, and in the way that people are reduced to soap motivations. The Croat writer Dubravka Ugrešić gave an example of how *poshlost* (the Russian version of kitsch) works:

> In his book about Gogol, Vladimir Nabokov uses the term *poshlost.* *Poshlost* is a Russian word which, because of its wealth of meanings, Nabokov prefers to English equivalents such as cheap, inferior, sorry, trashy, scurvy, tawdry and the like. By way of illustration of *poshlost* Nabokov takes Gogol's description of a young German. This German is paying court in vain to a young girl who spends each evening sitting on her balcony, knitting stockings and enjoying the beautiful view over a lake. Finally the German devises a strategy to capture the girl's heart. Every evening he undresses, dives into the lake and swims before the eyes of his beloved, while at the same time embracing two swans he has acquired especially for this purpose. In the end the young man wins the girl thanks to the witty notion of the swans.
>
> (Ugrešić 1998: 49)

The point is that while *poshlost* merely provokes a benign smile, as Nabokov pointed out, *poshlost* is 'particularly strong and pernicious when the falsity is not so obvious and when it is believed, rightly or not, that the values it imitates belong to the highest reaches of art, thought or sensibility'.

Since the time of the industrial revolution things have passed through transformation from 'transient–rubbish–durable' with increasing speed. But with the electronic age this process has speeded up considerably and has produced not only vast quantities of kitsch, but also whole industries based on kitsch (Thompson 1977: 42). In the 1970s Arthur Schlesinger Jr, part of the White House entourage, a close friend of President John F. Kennedy and member of the president's Brains Trust, applied the idea of kitsch to the USA. He pointed out that the incredible geographical mobility of the US population (every year 20 per cent of the population move house) and the intense consumerism of US society were major factors contributing to the power of kitsch (Alvarez 1965: 157). He also described the 'burnout' suffered by artists exposed to the mass media, and offered the example of the comedian. Half a century ago a comedian could be a success in vaudeville for twenty-five years with just two or three acts: now they would be out of material after a year in television. The speed at which material is used, recycled and dumped has increased alarmingly.

We may have reached the point where it is not even necessary to have written a novel before the publicity machine gets to work. Children's author Louisa Young has written:

Tragically I am no longer the New J. K. Rowling. I read in the paper that one Jonathan Stroud is the New New J. K. Rowling, and so my brief but glorious reign is over – before, I may say, the book that won me the title is even published. [. . .] You may think that being the New J. K. Rowling is an experience granted to few . . . but you'd be wrong. New J. K. Rowlings are ten a penny (which must be galling for the Actual J. K. Rowling). There was Georgia Byng, Eoin Colfer, Lemony Snicket, Loraine Kelly and that vicar, and the guy whose mother saved his manuscript from the bin. Recently the BBC held a contest for the position, which a drama student from Canterbury won. Even the AJKR was herself voted the NJKR in a poll.

(Young 2003: 20)

Kitsch encourages us to blur literary values into commercial values, to believe that what sells is good. And the more it sells the more brilliant it is. It encourages us to confuse lack of commercial success with artistic failure and, even if we cannot achieve originality, makes authenticity of expression, the next best thing, harder to spot.

Homogenization of markets

On TV in the USA and the UK, there is continuous pressure to produce anodyne adaptations of literary classics, cookery, travel, gardening, fly on the wall documentaries, public confrontation and confession shows, house makeovers, quizzes and cheap game shows – most of which make no great use of either writers or actors. And these shows have begun to displace sit-coms from prime time TV. There is also a 'feverish' market in buying and selling game show formats – not the shows, just the formats.

In the mid-1960s about a hundred new plays per year were broadcast on British TV. Each play reached an audience of 20–30 million viewers. Now, at most, the four major British TV channels produce a total of about sixteen new plays per year. Yet every TV soap takes up over fifty-two drama hours per year – some much more (http://bbc.co.uk/writers room/qanda/qandal; http://media.guardian.co.uk/rtscambridge/story). While it is claimed that since 1970 the broadcast output of 'TV Films and Drama' in the UK has risen enormously, 56 per cent of that increased output consists of repeats, and most of the remainder is imported from the USA. In 1994 UK TV spent £36,000,000 buying foreign programmes over what it earned from making and selling its own programmes abroad: by 1998 that figure had risen to £160,000,000 ('Television by numbers' 2001: 7). The fact is that, apart from adaptations of classic literature, very little new writing is commissioned for TV in the UK (Protheroe 2000: 4).

The situation is not much different in publishing. Writers have never had cause for confidence in publishers. Franz Kafka sold only a few stories in his lifetime: his first book had a print run of only 800; William Golding showed *Lord of the Flies* to twenty-one publishers before it was accepted; James Joyce offered *Dubliners* to thirty-two publishers; J. P. Donleavy took *The Ginger Man* to thirty-six. Italo Calvino could not find a publisher willing to take on his first book, *If This Is a Man*, so he arranged for it to be privately printed, initially in a print run of 200 copies. Even after the book proved successful, Calvino could not find a publisher willing to undertake a second edition.

In the UK a good print run for a literary novel is now 10,000 copies; the average hardback print run is less than 2,000 copies – even for a distinguished author. Sales of 1,000 copies indicate literary success. Even allowing for reprints, translations and paperback editions of classics, the UK still produces over 5,430 new novels per year, an average of 104 new novels per week. Since the late 1990s the number of novels published each year in the UK has risen by a staggering average of nearly 11 per cent per year to a total of 10,860 titles in 2000. In the year 2000 in the UK alone 112,000 new titles appeared, but of these fewer than 4,000 were reviewed, and only 154 sold more than 100,000 copies. Unless an author wins a prize, or has a very good advertising campaign behind them, most books do not sell even a hundred copies (Wagner 2002: 12).

After 1983, when Salman Rushdie won the Booker Prize, and the commercial success of Graham Swift's *Waterland* and Thomas Keneally's *Schindler's Ark* indicated a wave of public interest in 'the literary novel', publishers in the UK and USA became increasingly desperate to anticipate and even create the 'next big thing'. They began to offer enormous advances to writers against highly imaginative royalty predictions. There can now be little doubt that the failure of this strategy left publishers desperate to recoup these huge sums and in a poor position to resist the 'restructuring' that hit them in the late 1980s and early 1990s. In 1997 Random House wrote off $80,000,000 in unearned advances, and at about the same time HarperCollins wrote off $270,000,000 for the same reason. The transatlantic publishing take-overs of the early 1990s inevitably meant that literary tastes became further strait-jacketed by reducing the range of books that could be made available. In the USA, for example, there are over 53,000 publishers, but 93 per cent of the books are produced by just twenty companies; 2 per cent are produced by the university presses, and only 5 per cent come from the smaller independent presses. In the UK in 1987 fifty major publishers were responsible for more than 60 per cent of the books published, but with the industrial restructuring the UK example was brought into line with the US situation. This impacted on local bookstores: in the period 1990–2003 more than one in ten independent book-sellers in the UK went out of business, unable to compete with diminished profit margins and competition from the bookshop chains like Waterstones (*You and Yours* 2001; Moss 2002: 6).

The way books are reviewed does not help either. In the UK 30 per cent of the top hundred authors are reviewed by other authors in the top hundred. At the same time, the number of books returned unsold to the publishers has risen from 20 per cent in the 1960s to over 40 per cent in 2000. Over 10 per cent of all new books are now pulped within the first fifteen months of their existence: in the UK 25,000 books per day, 6,000,000 books per year, are sent for pulping. Popular literature, how-ever, does not suffer from these problems. In 2000, Thomas Harris's *Hannibal* sold 1,095,862 copies and grossed £7,660,075. Worldwide, romantic fiction sales are worth £70,000,000 per annum. Harlequin-Mills and Boon regularly sells over 2,000,000 books per annum world-wide, with UK print runs of 100,000 (Hamilton 2000: 10; Schiffrin 2000: 113, 126, 142).

James Woods believes that 'nobody tells the truth about contemporary literature'. And what is the truth? Woods has no doubt that most contempo-rary novels are poor, that 'they will not last beyond the flickering dream-life of their publication, that their writers should not have allowed them to appear, and that those writers are probably wasting their time writing at all' (Turner 1997: 204). The result has been dubbed 'market censorship' (Schiffrin 2000: 105). As Trevor Griffiths put it, now 'the marketplace is the great censor in the sky' (Griffiths 2001). This is the reality of contemporary literature, and since the collapse of communism this reality has become very nearly global.

Writing and marketing

The trend is to make no distinction between writing and other products, to allow the worlds of writing and marketing to 'interpenetrate' each other. In 1989 Stewart Home 'placed' 100 Pipers whisky in his novel *Pure Mania*, for which he was rewarded with a case of whisky from the distiller. Bill Fitzhugh's *Cross Dressing* took this a step further. The novel, which pur-ported to lampoon the advertising industry, blurred the distinction between literature and marketing by 'placing' Seagram's whisky as a named drink in the text. In itself this was a sound marketing strategy since Seagram's also owned Universal Studios, who bought the film rights to the book (Fitzhugh 2000: 27; Home 2000).

Publishers have begun to try using books as gifts even at the reviewing stage – presumably in the hope of influencing reviewers. The publisher

Fourth Estate, for example, sent review copies of David Flusfeder's *The Gift* out to literary editors with a wrap-around slip saying 'Signed First Edition'. The author had apparently been persuaded to sign 4,000 copies. Donna Tart was induced to sign 500 copies of her novel *The Little Friend*. And books have now begun to arrive on reviewers' desks complete with chocolates, balloons and T-shirts. Routledge sent out review copies of Raimond Gaita's *The Philosopher's Dog* with a cuddly toy mastiff. Reviews, it is widely acknowledged do not sell books and are largely irrelevant. But publicity, it seems, is different. That is essential (Seaton 2003: 6).

The last thing publishing wants is a publicity shy author. Now J. D. Salinger would be politely shown the door. If Golding's *Lord of the Flies* were to arrive on a literary editor's desk now, it would almost certainly have to offer a marketing package. It would probably be accompanied by a one-paragraph plot summary – 'It's like *The Coral Island*, but this island paradise is definitely lost, in fact it is a kind of underage *Hell in the Pacific*. It is populated by English choir boys – but these kids are like *Midwich Cuckoos*.' The author would probably supply a list of possible directors and big-name actors for the film adaptation (in truth the script is already half written), a list of 'Island Ideas' for a promotional holiday gimmick involving a leading tour operator, a list of glossy magazines to which review copies should go, a reassuringly youthful publicity photo of the author, a list of literary festivals at which the author might do high-profile readings, a sponsorship deal from a leading insecticide manufacturer and, for good measure, a warning-endorsement from a leading populist preacher, preferably including words like 'sin', 'evil', 'torture', 'darkness' and 'bestial'.

For a moment I thought I might be exaggerating just a little here, until I noticed this book advertisement on the back page of *The Guardian*:

> Batavia's Graveyard (Mike Dash) is utterly **absorbing,** an adult Lord of the Flies – Treasure Island meets Deliverance. *Evening Standard*
> (*The Guardian* 2003: 40)

Perhaps we are not quite there yet, but we are definitely on the way.

Publisher André Schiffrin has said that authors sell out, but publishers merely anticipate inevitable trends (Schiffrin 2000: 71). Certainly publishers are desperately searching for the next 'big thing', the next 'coming name', the next big break, the chance to sit back on a success story: consequently transatlantic publishing has a great many writers dropped after their first book. Modern publishing is a risk-averse industry, and it does not encourage an author to change the 'formula' that has produced sales in the past. Writing with mass appeal reproduces itself faster and sells more than literary genres. In this, writing is no different from anything else in nature.

The animal with the biggest range, the fastest breeding cycle, the widest diet, often succeeds in taking over a whole habitat and ecological niche from slower breeders and selective feeders (Brayfield 2001: 17). TV critic Mark Lawson has said that being an artist in the twenty-first century is like living in a listed building:

> You can only make minor changes because the original features are what people want to see. Where Shakespeare created his own *Troilus*, now Ridley Scott offers us his take on *Ben Hur*. The bias towards re-cycling ideas has been intensified by the way major movies, television shows and commercial novels are now commissioned. The 'pitch' is a reductive Hollywood tradition in which ideas are described in a few lines, inevitably referring to successful predecessors. It's *Harry Met Sally* but she's an alien, it's *Brief Encounter* but they're gay.
>
> (Lawson 2000: 22)

It is not that the cultural pessimists can argue for a decline in the quality and scope of the novel. Brilliantly original and inventive novels continue to be written in both the UK and the USA. It is not just that the collapse of the distinction between mass and literary fiction has left serious writers high and dry. What academic Harold Bloom called 'the anxiety of influence' might deter or inhibit the more intellectually aware writers from succumbing to their pet literary enthusiasms, or from following through lines of experimentation, but the populist writers have plundered what has gone before without hesitation (Bloom 1973; 1994). Difficult and innovative writers have always found it hard to get published, stay in print and carry on writing (Clark 2000: 20). The problem is that this situation, at a time of increasing globalization, aids standardization and does not encourage literary experiment, development or innovation:

> Creativity is, from its deepest instinct, intolerant: it is based on creative originality. I would even go so far as to say that the intolerance of the poetics of a literary work, the intolerance of its spiritual and aesthetic uniqueness, is the direct source of the vitality of literature as an art form. Every newly discovered style of poetics mercilessly buries the previous one, is bitterly inimical to it; the one denies the other, one lives from the death of the other. It is a struggle to decide the better. The only works that are tolerant are those that are eclectic, derivative, semi-inventive, conformist. Then literature endures as a kind of consumer good; it does not bother the reader with exclusive insurgency but simply, in its mediocrity, makes him or her feel like a consumer of literary quality, and allows its authors to rest comfortably in the

embrace of gentle waves, in which a great leap is reduced to pulp and
gradually flows into the net of literary boredom.

(Kanturkova n.d.: 183)

If more books are being published it is not that a wider range of novels,
plays and poetry is being produced in ever more challenging and adventur-
ous styles. It is simply that tastes have become much more clearly
'marketized'. More people are reading what market research and previous
sales reveal will sell. It is also because books about gardening, cookery, inte-
rior decoration, historical fiction, crime, thrillers, romantic and teenage
fiction are now the real backbone of Anglo-American publishing.

Novelist Jeanette Winterson calls this 'the golden calf in the wilderness'
syndrome. She has pointed out that it is part of the way we live, part of the
society we have created, and part of the cultural dilemma all contemporary
creative talent faces:

> Money culture recognizes no currency but its own. Whatever is not
> money, whatever is not making money, is useless to it. The entire
> efforts of our government as directed through our society are efforts
> towards making more and more money. This favours the survival of
> the dullest. This favours those who prefer to live in a notional reality
> where goods are worth more than time and where things are more
> important than ideas. [. . .] Money culture [. . .] must know what it is
> getting, when it is getting it, and how much it will cost. The most
> tyrannical of patrons never demanded from their protégés what the
> market now demands of artists; if you can't sell your work regularly
> and quickly, you can either starve or do something else. [. . .] Money
> confuses time with itself. That is part of its unreality. [. . .] Our
> increasingly passive diversions do not equip us, mentally, emotionally,
> for the demands that art makes. We know we are dissatisfied, but the
> satisfactions that we seek come at a price beyond the resources of a
> money culture. Can we afford to live imaginatively, contemplatively?
> Why have we submitted to a society that tries to make imagination a
> privilege when to each of us it comes as a birthright?

(Winterson 1995: 138)

Can writing be more than a hobby?

Writers of all kinds are blocked because they do not have access to the
levers of power or to money. How could it be otherwise? Publishing, films
and broadcasting are businesses: people do not invest in order to lose money.
The money men want guarantees. Writers are part of those businesses. The

technological revolution currently underway may make everyone their own desk-top publisher, but until the tail of the technological revolution catches up with the head, we have to ask about the connection between writing and money. This is not a vexed subject, merely embarrassing. We can only maintain fictions about fiction for so long. The question of money is a dirty one, but the fact is that we live in a world of harsh commercial values. Writers have all the other normal human responsibilities – to feed the kids, pay the rent, book a holiday, fix the car, sort out the TV licence, fetch the shopping – before they can begin to think of writing.

Where publishing and broadcasting are increasingly set on creating demands rather than satisfying need, the writer has to ask whether it is now possible to challenge the power of the mass market, the capacious maw of TV, the constricting power of publishers, the dead weight of tradition and the overwhelming pressure of kitsch?

Can writers make an effective challenge? Should they bother? Even if they do, there is no money in challenging the market. Not for a living writer. That much is certain. Should writers worry themselves about all this? Do they have a responsibility to be authentic or original? Do they have the opportunity? And if they are original will they be published or broadcast? No one in their right mind would question the idea that books have to sell. But equally there can be little doubt that many books do not sell simply because they are innovative, ahead of their time, say things which people are not ready to understand. Indeed, the more we know and understand about the lives of writers, the struggle they have to get original work taken seriously, the conditions writers are forced to deal with, the more questionable the whole notion of the accepted literary canon becomes. Inevitably the 'original' writer will appear as frustrated, blocked, intolerant of the 'set-up'. This is part of the price of being an artist, one of the reasons why 'serious' literature is the way it is. As Jeanette Winterson wrote:

> We make it as difficult as possible for our artists to work honestly while they are alive . . . and when they are too old or too dead, or too beyond dispute to hinder any more, we canonize them, so that what was wild is tamed, what was objecting, becomes Authority.
>
> (Winterson 1995: 11)

Self-publishing has always been the writers' answer to reluctant publishers. And it seems to be developing now as the only viable route for serious and innovative work. Writers who have been driven to self-publication include William Blake, Elizabeth Barrett Browning, Thomas Paine, Alfred Lord Tennyson, Charles Dickens, Lord Byron, Alexander Pope, Horace

Walpole, William Makepeace Thackeray, Robert Burns, Jane Austen, Honoré de Balzac, Alexandre Dumas, Edgar Allen Poe, Walt Whitman, Nathaniel Hawthorne, Virginia Woolf, Stephen Crane, e. e. cummings, Gertrude Stein, Rudyard Kipling, Beatrix Potter, John Galsworthy, Henry David Thoreau, Leo Tolstoy, Mark Twain, Upton Sinclair, W. H. Davies, T. S. Eliot, Ezra Pound, Ernest Hemingway, Lawrence Ferlinghetti, Marcel Proust, Benjamin Franklin, Zane Grey, Thomas Hardy, D. H. Lawrence, Carl Sandburg, George Bernard Shaw, Percy Bysshe Shelley, James Joyce, William Carlos Williams, Anaïs Nin, Margaret Atwood, Stephen King, Timothy Mo and Susan Hill. Roddy Doyle's *The Commitments* and Jill Paton Walsh's *Knowledge of Angels* (shortlisted for the Booker Prize) are among the most recent examples (Finch 1997: 19; http://www.bookmarket.com/self publish).

Technological advance now enables writers to self-publish to a standard of print and artwork that is almost identical with that on offer at the larger publishing houses. And the Internet is rapidly developing as a legitimate platform for new writing. One thing is certain: these opportunities bring writers a new responsibility – not to be blocked by existing publishers and by the constraints of the market. However, even if the growth of self-publishing and the possibilities of the Internet manage to by-pass conventional publishing, writers may still be falling into the modern version of starving in a garret since they are unlikely to make money from a web-site and do not have access to adequate publicity and distribution systems to sell books in large numbers.

The future

Perhaps the future lies in the post-modern writer-readership of one, in the cool, fragmented, virus free Internet chat-rooms, personal web-sites and interactive hypertext novels, and in on-line publishing, where every writer is their own perfect reader and perhaps the only reader. Romanian writer Norman Manea wrote:

> No matter how complicated, circuitous, or labyrinthine the artist's creative sources and resources may be, and no matter what spectacular exceptions could be put before me, I believe that the writer must fulfill his artistic obligations in his work, be severe with himself and with his vocation; as a public person he must remain, no matter what the price, exigent with himself and with society, responsible, in the best sense of the word, to truth and to society; he must become the honest conscience in which his fellow man can believe. In its sublime attempt to capture the ineffable essence of man and the cosmos, literature invents

its own laws, free of all authority outside its own standards for perfection. Artistic consciousness has to discover its echo, its validation, in a corresponding ethical consciousness. Let us not fool ourselves; it has never been easy to follow such a noble spiritual code. [. . .] The poverty, solitude, and lack of understanding that are a writer's lot seem at times easier to bear than the fact that he does not have access to the public forum, or that no one is interested in the opinion, good intentions, or the potential competence that he embodies.

(Manea 1994: 172)

These are fine, noble words, but they relieve literary agents, commissioning editors, publishers, broadcasters, cultural commentators, critics, reviewers, politicians, librarians, teachers and academics of the burden of cultural and political awareness and of intellectual and moral responsibility. They place the burden on the least influential person in western society. The real message of western cultural experience is no longer private and personal, but general and global. As Schiffrin puts it:

The idea that our society has been fundamentally affected by the importance of money is widely recognized. Other values that have been looked to as countervailing forces are fast disappearing. Not only our belongings but our jobs and, indeed, ourselves have become commodities to be bought and sold to the highest bidder. There have been other times in history when such changes have taken place. But now, linked to globalization and to the industrialization of the media, the effects are all the more staggering.

(Schiffrin 2000: 171)

What kind of a picture would emerge if we judged our literary culture on what writers had tried to say, on what had been ignored, sidelined, deemed unsaleable, on what it did not include, on what had not appeared, on what was not in print? Up to now we have judged our literary culture by what appears and survives. We are just at the beginning of the realization that the literary canon must also take account of what is not there, or what, if present in western culture, is almost invisible.

6   Censorship

Artists have always fought a battle with social mores and the powers that be. Artists are keen to push at the boundaries of the permissible, question the status quo and seek out the new. The authorities, on the other hand, tend to feel threatened by this and are generally inclined to enforce the boundaries of the permissible, support the status quo and suppress new ways of representing the world. While this is so in other art forms, it is much more so in writing and literature, where language is closely related to issues of identity and to political ambitions and competing ideas of community.

   The next chapter points out that writers now face a rapidly changing situation: censorship – at least in most 'western' countries – appears to be disappearing. It has become necessary to ask: What does the absence of censorship mean for the writer? Without censorship how is it possible for a writer to know which targets are important? In what ways might this affect a writer's sense of responsibility?

Censoring films

Although the USA trumpets freedom of speech very loudly, in reality the first amendment to the constitution, guaranteeing freedom of speech, religion, conscience and opinion, has been seriously compromised at every stage of its existence. Will H. Hays, one of the first US censors, linked entertainment, morality and race. He is reputed to have said: 'Correct entertainment raises the whole standard of a nation. Wrong entertainment lowers the whole living conditions and moral ideas of a race.' His thoughts on these things were enshrined in *The Production Code of the Motion Picture Producers and Distributors of America*. Even though it contravened the first amendment to the US Constitution, this code dominated the US motion picture industry throughout the 1930s.

   The Hays Code and its effects have been comprehensively documented.

In particular, during a period of Prohibition when organized violent crime was widespread, Hays was against the portrayal of the lives of real criminals unless they were shown being punished for their crimes. In the context of its time it is now possible to see that while the anti-communist witch hunts run by Senator McCarthy offered tight control over the people who made films, the Hays Code offered tight control of the films they made. Consequently the US motion picture industry through the 1940s was fearful, conservative and conventional.

The British Board of Film Censors came into being in 1914. In 1917, T. P. O'Connor, President of the Board, systematically and comprehensively laid down forty-three categories of material that could not be portrayed on British celluloid. The list, as a snapshot of Imperial Britain and the social and political controls used to maintain it, is instructive for writers:

1 Indecent, ambiguous and irreverent titles and subtitles.
2 Cruelty to animals.
3 The irreverent treatment of sacred objects.
4 Drunken scenes carried to excess.
5 Vulgar accessories in the staging.
6 The modus operandi of criminals.
7 Cruelty to young infants and excessive cruelty and torture to adults, especially women.
8 Unnecessary exhibition of underclothing.
9 The exhibition of profuse bleeding.
10 Nude figures.
11 Offensive vulgarity and impropriety in conduct and dress.
12 Indecorous dancing.
13 Excessively passionate love scenes.
14 Bathing scenes passing the limits of propriety.
15 References to controversial politics.
16 Relations of Capital and Labour.
17 Scenes tending to disparage public characters and institutions.
18 Realistic horrors of warfare.
19 Scenes and incidents calculated to afford information to the enemy.
20 Incidents having a tendency to disparage our Allies.
21 Scenes holding up the king's uniform to ridicule.
22 Subjects dealing with India in which British officers are seen in an odious light, and otherwise attempting to suggest the disloyalty of Native states, or bringing into disrepute British prestige in the Empire.
23 The exploitation of tragic incidents of war.
24 Gruesome murders and strangulation scenes.
25 Executions.

26   The effects of vitriol throwing.

27   The drug habit, e.g.: opium, morphia, cocaine, etc.

28   Subjects dealing with White Slave traffic.

29   Subjects dealing with the premeditated seduction of girls.

30   'First Night' scenes.

31   Scenes suggestive of immorality.

32   Indelicate sexual situations.

33   Situations accentuating delicate marital relations.

34   Men and women in bed together.

35   Illicit sexual relationships.

36   Prostitution and procuration.

37   Incidents indicating the actual perpetration of criminal assaults on women.

38   Scenes depicting the effect of venereal diseases, acquired or inherited.

39   Incidents suggestive of incestuous relations.

40   Themes and references relative to 'race suicide'.

41   Confinement.

42   Scenes laid in disorderly houses.

43   Materialization of the conventional figure of Christ.

('Empire of the censors' 1998: 10; Travis 2000)

Needless to say, if this list were in operation today very few contemporary films would achieve public viewing. A list of films and videos of the last forty years which have clashed with the British censor would include a great many now regarded as classics or at least as 'very important', including: *Psycho, Bonnie and Clyde, Easy Rider, Straw Dogs, A Clockwork Orange, Enter the Dragon, The Exorcist, Ai No Corrida, ET, Rambo, The Last Temptation of Jesus Christ, Cry Freedom, Reservoir Dogs, Thelma and Louise, Dumb and Dumber, Natural Born Killers, Independence Day, Schindler's List, Crash, Amistad, Tarzan, The World Is Not Enough, Saving Private Ryan, Austin Powers* (http://www.dtaylor.demon.co.uk/rejfilms; http://www.dtaylor.demon.co.uk/nasties).

However, the BBFC has over the last few years withdrawn from the role of censor and changed itself into a licensing authority. It is now less interested in policing moral conduct, upholding Christianity and the Empire, and expunging vernacular expletives, but much more concerned to monitor portrayals of violence, criminal behaviour, detailed criminal techniques and the illegal use of drugs. While it still monitors what it calls 'human sexual activity', and maintains a strict policy on sexual violence – 'rape, sexual assault, non-consensual restraint, pain or humiliation' – it now claims a much more enlightened general policy, stating that nudity without sex is 'acceptable at all classification levels'.

If anything, although the volume of visual material has increased through advances in video, CD and DVD technology, and the opportunities and capacity for intervention have increased massively, the BBFC cuts and censors films much less than it used to. In 1915, its first full year of operation, the BBFC censored one film, cutting 2.8 per cent. The high point of film censorship seems to have come in 1972–7, when the BBFC cut 28.7 to 33.9 per cent from 200 of the 600 films it licensed. By 2001, however, BBFC intervention had lapsed back to its 1915 level with cuts totalling a mere 2.8 per cent of the films it decided to control. In terms of statistics film censorship has come full circle (http://www.bbfc.co.uk/web site/Statistics).

Censoring books

In both the USA and the UK a surprising number of books by respected authors have triggered calls for suppression or censorship. As with films, a great number of these titles are now considered modern classics and it is hard to understand the nature of the offence they caused (Karolides *et al.* 1999). In the USA, although the First Amendment to the Constitution includes the right to read what you want, the area of what can or cannot be taught in schools or kept in a library is a moral and political battlefield. It has been estimated that in the USA in the year 1994–5 there were 458 attempts to remove books from libraries and school curricula. Of these, 169 – mainly in California, Texas, Pennsylvania and Oregon – were successful.

The book most frequently cited for suppression in the USA is Maya Angelou's *I Know Why the Caged Bird Sings*. Angelou is accused of having written a book which concentrates on 'lurid' sexual perversion and preaches hatred of whites. Similarly Mark Twain's *The Adventures of Huckleberry Finn* is often accused of bad grammar and racism for allowing characters to repeat so many racial slurs, and for failing overtly to reject slavery. Ironically when Twain's book first appeared it was accused of subverting slavery. Also among the top ten are John Steinbeck's *Of Mice and Men*, Judy Bloom's *Forever*, and J. D. Salinger's *A Catcher in the Rye*. The reasons for complaint vary. The Christian right inevitably objects to any and all portraits of non-conventional family life (*Attacks on the Freedom to Learn* 1996; Nugent 1996: 130; http://www.digital.library.upenn.edu/books/banned-books).

In the UK probably the most famous attempt to censor a literary work concerned D. H. Lawrence's novel *Lady Chatterley's Lover*. Lawrence had already had several brushes with the law over charges of obscenity. His novel *The Rainbow* had been seized and banned in 1915, his collection of poems *Pansies* had been massively cut by a scared publisher in 1929, and that same year an exhibition of his paintings had been seized by the police. Lawrence had written *Lady Chatterley's Lover* – a calculated full frontal assault on British attitudes to sex and sexuality – in 1928, but had been unable to publish it in Britain. He had first published it at his own expense in a private edition in Florence in 1929. However, when booksellers tried to import it, the book was seized by British Customs.

In the USA, the Customs Service declared the book obscene and prohibited it, and in 1930 a successful prosecution against a Yale librarian for illegally importing it provoked a national debate on public decency. In 1944 further copies of the book were seized and it was blacklisted by the National Organization of Decent Literature. In 1959 Grove Press produced the first unexpurgated edition of the novel but the Postmaster General banned it from the mails. Grove Press went to court and won, but later that year a new Postmaster General again banned the book.

In 1960 Penguin Books published an unexpurgated edition and was immediately prosecuted. At the Old Bailey trial no fewer than thirty-five distinguished writers, literary critics and teachers, including E. M. Forster, Dame Rebecca West, C. Day Lewis, Richard Hoggart, Graham Hough and Helen Gardner, gave evidence for the defence. The prosecution failed to find any writers or critics prepared to attack the book. They called only one witness, the detective inspector who had agreed to be the 'aggrieved complainant' – the person to whom the book was 'published'. The trial was over in less than five days (Rolph 1961).

Critics who warned of a tide of pornography bearing down upon civilization were only partly wrong. It has been said that the defeat of the *Lady Chatterley* prosecution led directly to the bare-chested page 3 girls in the UK newspaper *The Sun* from 1970 onwards. Perhaps it did. When they first appeared (and for a long time afterwards) it was said that these pictures were demeaning to women. Now, however, compared to what is currently available on TV, video and DVD and in the cinema, both *Lady Chatterley* and the page 3 girls seem tame, simplistic, middle of the road, naive, even cosy. If anything, both D. H. Lawrence and *The Sun* now appear rather conservative in their attitudes. That is not an argument in support of censorship, it is simply a measure of how much things have changed.

Does censorship protect us, or does it protect society from change? It may be that the British no longer need the kind of guidance the BBFC offered in the past. It may be also that the film-going audience is beginning to insist that it takes responsibility for itself. Certainly cinema audiences resent being manipulated or controlled in their pleasures. In March 2000, *Total Film* surveyed more than 2,000 readers on the subject of responsibility, film classification, the nature of allowable controversy and the range of censorship. The following is taken from their survey answers on 'the Question of Responsibility':

1   *The level of bad language in films is representative of bad language in everyday conversation.* No contest – a crushing 70 per cent thought that the effing and blinding up there on the screen was no worse than you get in the average chinwag on the street.

2   *It is the responsibility of the BBFC to protect young people from potentially damaging effects of viewing sex, violence and bad language in films.* Slightly less conclusive. Just over half of you thought the BBFC should be guarding the nation's youth from the horrors of film, while just under half thought the responsibility lay elsewhere.

3   *It is the responsibility of the cinemas and video retailers to protect young people from potentially damaging effects of viewing sex, violence and bad language in films.* 60 per cent think outlets should take greater responsibility for protecting the young.

4   *It is the responsibility of parents to protect young people from potentially damaging effects of viewing sex, violence and bad language in films.* More than 95 per cent rejected the notion that it's too much to expect parents to know what their kids are watching. Instead, you overwhelmingly believe that the responsibility lies with mum and dad.

5   *Classification exists to protect children, who are less able to distinguish between fact and fiction and more likely to be affected by powerful films.* But you do think that classification is useful in helping parents to decide: over 75 per cent thought ratings could help stop kids seeing films that might have a bad effect on them.

(*Total Film* 2000)

Censors as protectors

It is easy to portray censors as power-hungry control freaks and reactionary upholders of the status quo. It is also easy to set them in opposition to heroic, humanist, liberal writers intent only on searching out ever new artistic forms. The world (and particularly that of the arts) is never so simple. Censors make a great many assumptions about their work and their responsibilities. Many in the BBFC (perhaps most) are 'film buffs' who know a great deal about the business. And some, it is safe to assume, are frustrated writers. Many censors see themselves as moral guardians and think of themselves as resisting bad taste and exploitation. These are not features restricted to the UK: they were also characteristic of censors in the former communist states of eastern Europe ('Apparatus power' 1981: 55; Curry 1984; Tighe 1987).

Yet, for all its seriousness of purpose, there is something deeply patronizing about censorship, and something worrying about ideas that are not strong enough to withstand the glare of public debate. The more we learn about how censorship works the more we find that the deals struck behind the scenes are squalid and morally dubious. Before the first performance, Joe Orton was forced by the Lord Chamberlain to make changes to *Entertaining Mr Sloane*, but Penguin Books confounded the theatre censor by including the list of alterations when they published the play – books were not subject to the same powers or controls. Playwright David Hare has made the whole process of censorship appear absurd by describing how, when his play *Brassneck* (1975) was censored for TV, the Head of BBC Drama intervened to make an offer: 'I'll swap you two buggers for a shit' (Pike 1982: 42).

Censorship, its defenders say, seeks to protect society from the disconcerting and the unsettling, the unacceptable and the damaging. At one and the same moment, censorship also prevents the free circulation of ideas and information and the formulation of ambitions and feelings that lie outside the norm. It works to its own disadvantage by making a prize out of that which it seeks to reduce. The will to control how others think and feel is neither precise nor simple to effect. Nor can censorship operate in a predictable manner. As we have seen above, books and films judged by one generation to be obscene or pornographic are often judged by the next generation to be erotic and classic.

All systems of censorship, no matter how well grounded in the opinion of the moral majority or manipulated by the political ascendancy, are riddled with inconsistencies, impracticalities, contortions and contradictions, and bedevilled by the normal human hypocrisy of politicians, clerics, the police, the readers. The much publicized campaign by US writer Andrea Dworkin to get all pornography outlawed under US laws designed to suppress 'hate-speech' is an example of just how uncontrollable and unpredictable censorship can be. Although the US courts did not take her campaign seriously, the Canadian Government listened to what she said and then enacted a very stern code of censorship. However, the authors banned under the new law were not the pornographers she had been aiming at, but Maya Angelou, prominent liberal homosexual writers and Dworkin herself.

Censorship under communism

Censorship was the main and all-pervasive feature of the business of perception in the decaying Stalinist states of the eastern bloc. What the writers under the Stalinist system discovered very quickly was that a censored press, film industry and artistic community created a corrupted social life, and that the government and Party heard nothing but its own voice. Censorship, rather than helping to smooth the path of social and economic progress, actually suppressed legitimate grievances and set up a propaganda of success which was contradicted by everyday experience. This very quickly bred a demoralizing cynicism and antagonism towards the state which society had no way of satisfying, diverting or even easing. It also created a desperate hunger for the things censored, an underground market for rumour, paranoia and misinformation.

One of the effects of censorship under communism, and one which writers continually struggled against, was that it made the feelings and thought processes of human discovery and cognition increasingly difficult and irrational. Censorship blocked channels of information and feeling within society and in individuals. By 1989, after nearly half a century of communist rule, not only did the societies of east-central Europe no longer know what they thought or felt about themselves or the world, they didn't know that they no longer knew.

The withdrawal of censorship, the freedom to think and say and do just what you liked, was an even more dizzying experience and totally disorienting for the writers of the former Soviet bloc. For forty-five years they had known what they were against and where their main opponents were to be found. Now they did not know the shape of their world, did not know who they were against or where their enemies were. The speed of the change, and the sudden silence of their writers, made the shock of 'liberation' into democracy, the sudden proximity of the multinational, multiethnic west and the tantalizing nearness of capitalist consumer items on the 'free' market very difficult to cope with.

Writers and censorship

Writing about sex and/or violence imposes certain obligations and limitations on every writer. Most writers are aware of a range of limitations on what they can and cannot do – and these are social limitations rather than formal censorship, but no less effective for being so. Writers in general do not jeer or sneer at the unfortunate, glorify cruelty or foster race hate. And in these things they are a positive force for good. But sometimes the issues are not easy to grasp or write down. Since *Lady Chatterley's Lover*, writing about sex raises the problem of what details to leave out, as much as what details to include. Indeed, in film and TV writing, it has become increasingly difficult to distinguish between pornography and serious writing with a sexual or violent content.

The novelists Kingsley Amis and Elizabeth Jane Howard, while aware that self-censorship could be as damaging as any imposed censorship, evolved a rough code of conduct, formulated from their own experience, to deal with these issues:

1   Directly sexual matter should not be introduced gratuitously, without reason in subject, character, story or plot. The discerning reader will detect it immediately as cheapening.

2   Writers should not be led astray by false notions of manly (or womanly?) frankness, determination to call a spade a spade, refusal to be bound by 'outmoded' convention, or – a more insidious one, responsible for who knows how many pages of relentless detailed description – fear of being thought shy or ashamed or guilty or 'hung up' about sex.

3   Nothing which the discerning reader will detect as the product of sexual excitement should be passed for publication. It is neglect of this restraint which can so much heighten the embarrassment of the reader. [. . .] If a writer seeks private relief by committing his fantasies to paper, that, again, is his affair. But he will be well advised to see to it that it remains so. Publication will alienate the discerning reader and, to a degree, bring serious writing into disrepute.

4   A qualifying clause: restraint does not mean suppression. The reader should be left in no doubt as to, at any rate, the outline of what took place at any given sexual encounter, provided [. . .] that it is relevant to other parts of the book. The most elementary skill is sufficient to satisfy this requirement.

5   Four letter words in their root meanings are to be avoided. Today, nearly half a century after *Lady Chatterley's Lover* was written, their associations in print remain either comic or brutal or both. Their use in dialogue for such effects is (we feel) inoffensive. Not moral delicacy, but the simple law of diminishing artistic returns, decrees that such use be occasional.

This last precept may seem very much a matter of taste. So indeed it is, and so are all the others. The notions of good taste, having at one period been used to justify much unthinking snobbery and priggishness, have understandably dropped out of fashion if not of mind. But, often concealed from view, they lie at the heart of this whole debate, and it is the impossibility of legislating to ensure the one and to banish the other which has caused so much confusion among those who have interested themselves in the matter.

(Amis and Howard 1972: 150)

These writers were at pains to point out that debate in this area often came down to a matter of taste and that political thought, artistic inclination, literary preference, the language of the streets, opinions on sex, social change and the use of violence could be socially negotiated. They were also keen to point out that as language usage and social mores were in constant flux, they could not be effectively regulated by law.

But censorship comes in many forms and it is as well to remember that Alexander Solzhenitsyn was censored by expulsion from the USSR, that death threats made against Salman Rushdie were an attempt not only to punish him for daring to think his own thoughts, but to silence him for the future, and that the execution of Nigerian playwright Ken Sara Wiwo, who protested at the ecological damage to Ogoni territory by the Nigerian Government and the multinational oil companies, was an attempt to silence a whole people who had something to say about the ecological damage worked not only on their homeland, but upon the whole planet.

Censorship in retreat

Now in the UK it is possible to write, publish, broadcast and read a great deal more than at any time in the last sixty years. Nude magazines are, by common consent, simply placed on the higher shelves in newsagents' shops. UK Channel 5 regularly shows soft porn films. In November 2000 the French film *Romance* was shown on UK television and erections made their first TV appearance in Britain. At about the same time the BBFC licensed the Danish film *The Idiots*, which showed sexual penetration from the point of view of the penis. Had theatre censorship operated in the UK after 1968, plays like Brenton's *The Romans in Britain*, Nichols's *Passion Play*, Kushner's *Angels in America*, Stoppard's *The Real Thing*, Pinter's *The Lover* and *Landscape* could not have been staged. Now it is very difficult to frame any form of control that will be relevant for more than a few months. The advent of home video, multichannel TV (there are more than forty stations available in the UK), the Internet and the creation of hundreds of local radio stations indicate a pattern of fragmentation that defies control (*Censored/Banned* 1996).

Censorship may pervert a culture, but victory over censorship is often hollow. Even the most high-minded literary ambition can be turned into something else. Forty years ago, when *Lady Chatterley's Lover* was put on trial, there were no aboveground erotic publishers in Britain. A reader seeking out materials by Lawrence, Joyce or Henry Miller had to order books from Paris and, in the UK, run the risk of prosecution if the Post Office discovered what was in the parcel. Today there are dozens of erotic publishers, many of them offshoots of major publishing concerns: New English Library, Liaison and Delta (all from Hodder Headline), Black Lace and Nexus (both from Virgin), X Libris (from Little, Brown and Co.),

Temptation (from Mills and Boon), Eros Plus (from Titan Books), Silver Moon Books, Classic Erotica (from Wordsworth), and Grove Press. Lawrence's highly original and challenging *Lady Chatterley's Lover* took thirty-four years to get into print with a major publisher, and it spawned a repetitive and desperately unadventurous multi-million dollar industry.

However, the fact remains that these changes represent parts of a long struggle to wrest culture from the hands of an elite. The worst that can be said about the literary culture we have created since the collapse of the *Lady Chatterley* prosecution is that it is increasingly commercial, rather than artistic in its motivation. The printed word, theatre, film, radio and TV, each at one time the site of an intense battle for cultural, religious and political control, have in their turn been commoditized, repackaged and marketed. And as this has happened, it has become clear that each has ceased to be a threat to the establishment, has ceased to be an object of interest for the would-be controllers, and is no longer a real case for censorship. That censorship has relaxed its grip on areas of creativity is a good thing, but it is also an indication that these areas are no longer as powerful, innovative or exciting as they once were and that they are no longer a danger to established power structures. What the collapse of censorship tells us is that real power has shifted elsewhere.

But if literary culture itself is no longer a site of significant conflict about society, and is no longer worth controlling, what is? If censorship does not tell the writers where the pressure points are, how will they know what is worth defending or attacking? In the future, it seems, writers must be responsible for seeing, identifying and defining these things for themselves. Again and again.

7 Political correctness

This chapter looks at some of the effects of political correctness (PC) on writing and writers. This is a difficult area and one which affects writers directly since, if political correctness is strictly applied (and it always intends this should be the case), it impinges on the areas of language writers can employ, the subject matter they can write about and even the characters they can use.

This chapter asks: To what extent must we mind our language, not just in swearing but in ordinary everyday speech and writing? Are writers prepared to fight to retain access to the entire range of the language? Or, if PC reductionism is a good cause, are they prepared to settle for access to just part of the language? What should writers do if they want characters in their stories who are not of the same gender, sexual persuasion, colour and race as themselves?

The political correctness movement

Although the phrase 'political correctness' came from Mao Tse Tung's *Little Red Book*, the political correctness movement sprang up in the USA in the late 1960s and grew rapidly (Dunant 1994). It developed out of a debate within American university campus culture, and addressed the complex issue of how we unconsciously discriminate against certain kinds of people by embedding discrimination in the way we speak and write. It attempted to find linguistic routes by which people would not be labelled pejoratively. Thus someone who was small was *vertically challenged*, or a *person of diminished stature*; bald men became *follicly challenged* or *hair disadvantaged*; fat people were said to be *possessing an alternative body image*; people were neither crippled nor disabled, they were *differently abled*; blind people became *visually impaired*; slums became *inner city areas*, poor people became *disadvantaged*; drunks became *chemically inconvenienced*, drug addicts became *drug dependent*;

prostitutes became *sex workers, sex care providers* and *physical welfare workers*; evil became *morally different* (Beard and Cerf 1992).

The idea was based on sound humanitarian principles and was something which the left (feminism, multiculturalism and anti-racist movements in particular) felt proud of. But it had a runaway life of its own. It soon became a well-meaning authoritarianism, working on a phobic knee-jerk reaction to certain sounds or verbal formulations without regard to historical meaning, context, intent or the application of the speaker. The tendency was to make a fetish of certain words, so that even a discussion *about* the word, the history or changing meanings of the word, could not take place. Some universities, supposed to be bastions of free speech and guardians of intellectual liberty, were so plagued by the problems of PC that they had to take legal action to free themselves. The PC movement was characterized by its critics and opponents as a new McCarthyite witch hunt, and as an Orwellian attempt to control thought and speech. There are numerous court rulings against political correctness as an infringement of the first amendment to the US Constitution, the guarantee of freedom of speech and thought.

PC and race

After the ending of slavery in the US, in polite white usage, black people became *darkies, colored folks* or *colored people*, then later they became *negroes*, then in the 1960s they became *blacks* or *black folks*, and then in the 1980s they became *African-Americans*. Recently there has been a tendency to refer to them as 'persons of color' (again). As if people who were not *of color*, were see-through. And in rap music there is no doubt they have become *niggaz* again. The words may have changed, but for millions of white Americans, from the time of George Wallace (Governor of Alabama) to that of David Duke (Grand Wizard of the Ku Klux Klan), these people were always 'niggers': the shift of names did not alter the facts of racism or the condition of their lives. The notion that it was possible to change a situation by finding a nicer word to describe it emerges, as art critic Robert Hughes pointed out, from the old American habit of euphemism, circumlocution, and 'desperate confusion about etiquette, produced by the fear that the concrete will give offence'. Hughes is certain that no shifting of words would ever reduce bigotry (Hughes 1994: 19).

It has not been socially permissible for a white person to use the words *negro* or *nigger* (with good reason) for some years. But it is particularly important, if you want to chart race relations in America, the history of the anti-slavery movement, the history of jazz and blues music, urban and industrial development or the history of the KKK to be able to see and understand these shifts in language, and use these words, as they represent shifts in understanding. However, under the influence of PC it has become very difficult to use these words at all, even in a sourced quotation, or as part of a discussion about language. Effectively these words became taboo for many people.

When I worked at Manchester City College in the late 1990s, staff were issued a circular which said it was no longer possible to use the word *black-board*, as this was racially offensive. We should instead use *white board* or *chalkboard*. The idea was so powerful, and its supporters so insistent, that nobody seemed to notice the board itself had no race and as an inanimate object could not take offence. That calling it a *white board* might have been equally racist does not seem to have occurred to anyone. And people who tried to enforce this rule, while they were happy to refer to white people by the confusing term *Caucasian*, tied themselves in knots over what to call the *blackbirds* hopping around outside the window.

The language of colour, when applied to people, is always a metaphor aimed at something other than colour. In race relations colour is at best an unsatisfactory metaphor. It indicates things which are, it is felt, somehow socially agreed: red, white, yellow, black. These things are supposed to have meaning. However, the explorers who set out from Europe were not the colour of paper; the people of the orient are not the same colour as daffodils; the tribes of the new world were never the same colour as rubies; the people of Africa were not the same colour as coal. People, it seems, are rather like grapes: white grapes are not white and black grapes are not black.

PC circumlocution

The word *man* was another early PC target. English derives part of its word hoard from Anglo-Saxon, a Germanic language in which *mann* means *person* rather than *male*. But over history while *man* included the whole of humanity, *man* also developed as meaning male. Of course it is possible to make this distinction in a university, but on the street both words are said and written the same way, and there is very little to be gained from giving a lecture on linguistic history every time you use the word. In practice most people assume that *man* is male and in certain circumstances includes female. Clearly for feminists this was a situation that needed addressing. *Man* soon became *humanity*, which may have been close to its original meaning but which left *man* un-housed and outside civilized conversation.

Chairman soon became *chairperson*. However, the use of the suffix *person* actually defeated itself because males were often referred to as *chairman*, and sometimes as *the chair*, they were rarely *chairperson*; women became the only candidate for *chairperson*. When it came to *manning* the office, *manual* labour, *manhole* covers, the argument ran that the *man* element in these words should be replaced with *person* or by *human*. Thus we should *person the office*, do *human labour* or *personlabour*, and have *humanholes* or *personholes*. These clearly make little sense and offered a very different meaning.

Euphemisms are a major part of PC. Robert Hughes has complained about the impact of PC euphemism and circumlocution in Australia:

> Recently I was sent the Australian Government's Style Manual for official publications, which forbids, among other things, such terms as *sportsmanship, workman, statesmanlike*. [. . .] Even *craftsmanship* is out; its mellifluous alternative is 'skill application'. Soon my fellow-countrymen, persuaded by American examples to look for euphemisms where no insults exist, will rewrite *Waltzing Matilda* to begin 'Once a jolly swag-person camped by a billobong.'
>
> (Hughes 1994: 19)

But it happens in the UK too. In the *Parliamentary Report on Fox Hunting* (June 2000) it was said that fox hunting could not be said to be cruel because the fox died quickly, nevertheless 'it tended to be detrimental to the well-being of the fox'. This is laughably wide of the mark – or would be if it did not disguise the fact that one animal is being torn apart by others.

Political correctness is also responsible for extending our range of *isms*: we now have, among many others, *sexism, ageism, ableism, racism*. And alongside these we have the associated adjectives ending with *ist: sexist, ageist, ableist, racist*. All of which, if you will pardon the euphemism, are stylistically challenged.

PC addresses the outward forms of language without understanding the way language works as a social phenomenon, mediating reality. It takes no account of historical content or historical context. It is concerned only with the outward appearance or sound of a word, perhaps only its form or spelling, not its history, its historically derived meaning, the changes that might have taken place in its usage, or changes in its context. Each of these is a serious refusal to deal with the nature of language.

Novelist and essayist George Orwell anticipated something of this development and warned that this kind of political alteration destroyed language without addressing the situation it described. The only safeguard against this demolition, he argued, was to see all political language for what it was – 'designed to make lies sound truthful and murder respectable, and to give an appearance of solidity to pure wind'. We cannot, he assured us, change all this in a moment, but we could at least change our own writing and reading habits (Orwell 1986b: 156).

Representing reality in language

While PC affected the language, the way things and people were described, it did nothing to alter reality. And this came to irritate the people it was supposed to protect. At New Year 2000, UK Channel 4 showed a brief feature in which a man asked not to be called *visually impaired* saying he preferred to be referred to as blind: 'My sight is not impaired. I can't see. I am blind. Saying my sight is impaired is inaccurate, it implies my sight is not perfect. This is so wide of the mark it is actually insulting, even damaging.' And there is evidence to suggest that some 70 per cent of black Americans prefer to be called *black* rather than the approved politically correct term, *African-American* (Crystal 1995: 177).

Political correctness is a serious attempt to right wrongs by altering the language in which those wrongs are presented and preserved. For example in response to the charge of institutional racism levelled at all British police forces in the late 1990s, the Greater Manchester Police Appropriate Language Working Party produced a document entitled *The Power of Language*, covering 'issues of race, disability, gender, religion, sexuality and age'. This publication listed a number of common idiomatic phrases no longer deemed appropriate for the police to use including: *old codger, old biddy, old fool, deaf and dumb, wheelchair bound; paki, negro, nigger, coon, wog, non-white; cretin, spastic, cripple, mongol, people with special needs; happy clappy, Bible basher, God botherer, God Squad; queer, poofter, fag, dyke, butch, gays; often do those kinds of jobs, a woman with lesbian tendencies, a person of the other persuasion, he/she bats for the other side*. The report was at once welcomed by the UK Commission for Racial Equality (*The Power of Language* 2000). The Metropolitan Police (covering the London area) does not maintain a list of banned words, but does maintain what it calls a Tolerance Code. It urges its officers to make sure that 'the language they use would not cause offence' and while it warns that Metropolitan Police officers breaching the Tolerance Code may face disciplinary proceedings, the force admits that what might give offence is, in the end, subjective.

However, the effect of importing PC concerns into policing, while it curbed expressions of racism, made language itself a minefield. For example, in 2002 a row broke out when Home Office Minister John Denham used the phrase 'nitty gritty'. His audience, from the Police Federation, pointed out that they were not allowed to use words like that. Although he did not know it, the word had its origins in the slave trade and referred to the debris left behind when the slaves were removed from the slave ship's hold after a transatlantic voyage. His audience also pointed out that the phrase 'a good egg' was not allowed since it was too closely associated with 'egg and spoon', which was rhyming slang for 'coon'. While good intentions cannot be doubted, the effect of such considerations was to hamstring vernacular language and make speakers of all political persuasions very nervous of saying anything. Political correctness achieved this without affecting the basic issues at all (Kettle 1999; Younge 2000b; Buruma 2001; Hopkins 2002)

Addressing important issues

To say that someone is short, bald, blind, old, lesbian, black, disabled may now be socially questionable, and there may be better ways of describing people. To change to *wheelchair user* rather than *confined to a wheelchair* may be progress of a sort, but it does not change the fact of the person's situation, nor does it really do much to change the problems a wheelchair user has in getting about in a wheelchair-unfriendly society:

> We want to create a sort of linguistic Lourdes, where evil and misfortune are dispelled by a dip in the waters of euphemism. Does the cripple rise from his wheelchair, or feel better about being stuck in it, because someone back in the days of the Carter administration decided that, for official purposes, he was 'physically challenged'? Does the homosexual suppose others love him more or hate him less because he is called a 'gay'? The net gain is that thugs who used to go faggot bashing now go gay-bashing. [. . .] We do not fail, we underachieve. We are not junkies, but substance abusers; not handicapped, but differently abled. And we are mealy-mouthed unto death: a corpse, the *New England Journal of Medicine* urged in 1988, should be referred to as a 'nonliving person'. By extension, a fat corpse is a differently sized nonliving person. If these affected contortions actually made people treat one another with more civility and understanding, there might be an argument for them. But they do no such thing.
>
> (Hughes 1994: 19)

Columnist Gary Younge has pointed out that to label someone politically correct is to make us suspicious of them. PC calls up a particular kind of linguistic nit-picking obfuscation, a fudging of issues beneath a relabelling of problems. PC has become a particularly useful rhetorical device for right-wing politicians who aim to brand their opponents as pedantic, controlling, ridiculous and misguided: the politics of the left is often referred to as PC so that it can be knocked down, put in its place. Indeed, he adds, to say someone or something is PC is a slur directed at all those who seek both to extend equality and to express it in their daily lives:

It is now used to deride just about anything conservatives either don't agree with – such as women-only short lists or non-smoking policies – or simply don't like. [. . .] In fact it has become so widespread it is virtually meaningless; an excuse for sloppy thinking aimed at anything which embraces or enhances diversity or, worse still, an excuse for not thinking at all.

(Younge 2000a: 17)

Gary Younge has estimated that the phrase *political correctness* occurs in British newspapers ten times more often than references to other political keywords like *regional policy, housing action, single parents* and *child poverty*. He cites the example of the British judge, Graham Boal QC, who in a speech at the Criminal Bar Association annual dinner in London in 1999 said the ideal candidate for promotion to the legal profession would now have: 'the breasts of a lesbian, the backside of a homosexual and a large black penis'. This was clearly a joke directed at minorities, but it was also aimed at PC.

Labelling something as 'politically correct' is not always sensible. There is an odd assumption that the UK and the USA have fallen under the spell of the loony liberal left, and that political correctness dominates their thinking. It is more likely that the opposite is true. If we lived in a PC world we would have many more frustrated writers, more neutered books, a much poorer TV culture, and a great deal more linguistic circumlocution. The right wing in the UK and the USA have appropriated, translated and mischievously employed the term to stigmatize all liberal left opposition. And the liberal left has often done itself few favours. But PC is a fake target. No major political or literary figure in either country defends PC. On the liberal left PC has been 'seen through' since the mid-1980s. Although PC still has a *few* adherents in the UK, and it has been influential in race relations, discrimination and equal opportunities legislation, it never really caught on. However, it is *referred* to so often in the UK that writers still have to be wary of it, and wary of those who criticize things as 'politically correct' since their opinions may be as reactionary and bigoted as the phantoms they seek to attack.

PC and writers

So, in practical terms, how does PC affect writers? One of the main problems is that PC seeks to introduce political considerations into purely literary matters. True, literature is political, and cannot avoid being part of the way we represent our world, but to do that effectively it must be free to show everything it needs to show. Creativity of all kinds has always been a major focal point for cultural exchanges and cross-fertilization. However, PC operates to limit the choice of subject matter, language, treatment and characters available to a writer by limiting imagination and decreeing ownership of experience. For example a hard-line feminist may use PC to object to a male writer using a first person female narrator in a story or voice over. The same feminist may also object to certain female experiences (female orgasm, childbirth, rape, domestic violence) being written about by male writers – even where this is done sensitively and responsibly. A white writer with a black narrator would probably invite the comments that (a) a white person cannot know anything for sure about this area of experience, and (b) this is just another form of intellectual colonialism, or to put it bluntly, theft of an experience and an identity.

PC alerts us to a whole range of issues affecting writers (Garner 1997). We may not live in a PC world, it is true, but for practising artists, PC should make us rather uneasy because it attempts to censor and repackage reality. As writers we have to ask ourselves whether, if we wrote politically correct stories, they might not be neutered to the point of being at best boring and at worst totally unreadable. In the recent past gay men and women have sought to prevent straight men and women from writing about them, and black people have sought to prevent white people writing about them (however responsibly), on the grounds that any writing by a straight white writer would be bound to patronize, misinterpret or misrepresent them, and that such writing would be an attempt by the white middle classes (particularly males) to steal another's experience yet again in order to make money out of it.

PC and the theft of experience

PC would prevent us from 'stealing' other historical experiences, but in doing so it would also prevent us from ever exposing or espousing someone else's cause in an artistic and imaginative way. It would operate to prevent imaginative sympathy with the experience of other lives. For example the jazz singer Billie Holiday is famous for several songs she made 'her own', but perhaps her most powerful and dramatic statement about the position of black people in the southern states of the USA is in 'Strange Fruit', which she first recorded in 1939, when she was twenty-three years old. At the time, although slavery had ended nearly a hundred years before, blacks and whites still lived in segregation. In spite of the fine words of the US Constitution about all men being born equal, the law did not apply equally to blacks and whites. Lynch law, supported by the Ku Klux Klan, connived at by local police forces, was the reality for southern blacks. As the Civil Rights movement got under way in the 1960s, this privilege was extended to white Civil Rights workers, as shown in the film *Mississippi Burning*. The opening lyric of 'Strange Fruit' is:

Southern trees bear a strange fruit
Blood on the leaves, blood at the root
Black bodies swing in the southern breeze
Black bodies hanging from the poplar tree

Although Billie Holiday claimed a hand in the writing, the song was actually penned by 'Lewis Allen'. This was the pen name of Abel Meeropol, a radical left-wing Jewish school-teacher in New York's Bronx. In 1938 he had seen a photograph of a lynching, wrote a poem about it for his wife, and then set the poem to music. He had taken the song to Billie Holiday and sung it for her while she was playing at a Jewish-owned night club in New York.

The song was a more accurate reflection of the place of blacks in US society than the film *Gone with the Wind*, and every bit as powerful as Ralph Ellison's novel *The Invisible Man*, and was a much more emotive anthem than the dreary 'We shall Overcome'. There had never been anything like this song before. There has been nothing like it since. Because they feared the 'race angle', Columbia Records refused to record it. It was eventually recorded by Jewish entrepreneur Milt Gabel on his privately owned Commodore label. Even then, very few radio stations would play the record, and only a few clubs would allow Billie Holiday to sing it. Understandably, if she sang the song, Holiday always made it the last in her set. If she sang 'Strange Fruit' she did not return for an encore. The song was very closely identified with her, and she was very possessive about it. When Josh White began singing it she is said to have pulled a knife on him. But since then it has been recorded by several artists including Nina Simone and Sting.

There is a very clear connection here between Jewish song-writing talent and black American music – a connection born out elsewhere too: Irving Berlin and Ira Gershwin both made extensive use of black American music. The black American experience seems to have coincided with Jewish experience of the ghettos of eastern Europe. The two cultures found and spoke to each other, exploring connections in music that we are only now beginning to understand. And this connection has been very important to the development of contemporary popular music. Without this connection opening up a 'space', it is unlikely that Elvis Presley, Motown, Soul, The Rolling Stones, The Beatles and Rap could have happened.

There is more to the song than musical history. Lynching has almost disappeared and the power of the Ku Klux Klan seems to have waned in favour of other, perhaps more subtle forms of racism, but the song, which in the end is not just about lynching but also an expression of race hate and intolerance, is still with us. 'Strange Fruit' is still powerful because we know that race hate still exists (Bosnia, Kosovo, Zimbabwe, South Africa, Rwanda), and because we know humans everywhere are still capable of behaving this way.

Is there any other way for us to understand ourselves and each other, apart from taking an imaginative leap into the life of another? Humanity, history and art are made from connections such as those the birth of this song illustrates. Art is made across barriers of race, gender, sexual preference and colour, and is often made in spite of barriers. Yet according to the tenets of political correctness, it is inappropriate for one race or gender or colour or sexual preference to speak of, or through, or about, another. What a rich experience and understanding PC would deny us.

Strategies of offence

It is not just that having a narrator who is other than the writer in any way may be politically incorrect, it is also that having characters other than the writer in a story, or even having references to them in 'ordinary' (incorrect) language, may be unacceptable. In effect what PC says is that the only experience you may write about is your own or that of people like you in every way. PC is not a recipe for interesting discussion, for accurate observation of the world, for sympathy, for understanding, for challenging the way the world is. It is not an effective tool in writing. André Brink has said that all significant art is offensive, and that sex, race and colour are but examples of the way in which literature 'offends'. But he has also warned that strategies of 'offence' involve much more than just the effort to offend.

> A literature which does not constantly and insistently confront, affront, offend – and thereby explore and test and challenge – the reader and the world, is moribund. If language is one of humanity's major instruments in its search for truth, its very nature demands of the writer never to cease from exploration – and to persist particularly when the offence it causes leads to a destructive system of countermeasures aimed at 'protecting' the weaknesses of the world. (In a society like South Africa the very threat of prosecution may suggest to the writer that he is heading in the right direction!) Part of the writer's responsibility to language, and to society which has provided him with it, lies in resisting every obstacle set up in the way of his exploration. However daunting may be the truth emerging from his work he has to

learn to live with it, and to live up to it, rather than look for shelter behind the walls of taboo. [. . .] In the act of offence we glimpse the possibility of freedom. As long as people can be offended by literature there remains a chance that they may be awakened from sleep in order to learn to face their world anew.

(Brink 1983: 119)

To do this writers need to cross boundaries, to transgress borders, to think themselves out of their own skin and deal imaginatively with issues, people, characters that are not 'us' and situations that are clearly not 'ours'. The question is whether increasing sensitivity towards potentially offensive material, and increasing sensitivity to language, might not curtail freedom to write and represent the reality of the world, with all its tragedies, comedies, bigotry and contradictions. Novelist John Berger has spoken of the difficulties of avoiding clichés in the attempt to render 'reality' in writing:

Reality, however one interprets it, lies beyond a screen of clichés. Every culture produces such a screen, partly to facilitate its own practices (to establish habits) and partly to consolidate its own power. Reality is inimical to those with power. All modern artists have thought of their own innovations as offering a closer approach to reality, as a way of making reality more evident. It is here, and only here, that the modern artist and revolutionary have sometimes found themselves side by side, both inspired by the idea of pulling down the screen of clichés which have increasingly become unprecedentedly trivial and egotistical.

(Berger 1984: 72)

It would seem that far from being a revolutionary attempt to alter 'reality', which is what it set out to be, PC has become a cliché behind which 'reality' remains resolutely unaltered. Yet, as writers, still we have to ask: In what ways is our freedom of vision and expression, our ability to represent the world as it is, to tell a good story and create interesting (but not necessarily 'nice') characters, limited by concern for others? Steve Bell, a UK political cartoonist of great originality and wit, never knowingly fettered by good taste, has written:

Pictures are no different from words because they can convey all sorts of meanings, both intentional and unintentional, and can be manipulated endlessly. Images are powerful and should not be sacred. Wrestling with them inevitably flies in the face of good taste and received wisdom. [. . .] It's a dirty job but somebody's got to do it. If everybody agreed with everyone about everything and offensive imagery were firmly under control it would be a sure sign that we were all dead from the neck up.

(Bell 1999: 191)

Political correctness for all its well-meaning folly asks an important question of each and every writer and reader. What extra-literary factors do we bring to bear when we read and judge a book? Is it important that in spite of the difficulties a book was nevertheless written and certain things were made clear that had not been revealed before? Is the ethnic, racial and sexual identity of the writer the real focus and limit of our interest? Are the marks of authentic victimhood a guarantee of literary quality?

Part 2

Case studies

8   New kinds of sex

J. G. Ballard, *Crash*

> The car and its connection to sex have been a major topic for pop songs since the 1950s. It is no accident that 'parking' is a major item on the US teenage social agenda. But where is the connection between cars and sex headed? Does the car promote the possibility of new kinds of sex? And what role do writers have in alerting us to changes in the human psyche?
>
> This chapter addresses these questions through a case study examination of J. G. Ballard's controversial novel *Crash*. It also revisits the issues of political correctness, originality and censorship.

Henry Ford (1863–1947) launched his 'horse-less buggy' in Detroit in 1893. In 1908 he launched the Model T Ford and initiated the first mass production assembly line shortly afterwards. His rate of expansion was prodigious: in 1909 the Ford company made 10,600 cars per year at a profit of $3,000,000; in 1914 they made 248,000 cars per year and profits soared to $25,000,000. By 1925 Ford had sold over 15,000,000 cars, his factory was producing 10,000 cars every twenty-four hours and he was probably the richest man in the world (Canning 1965: 283). Since then the car has had a major impact on all areas of human existence, and while its effect on towns, planning, health, economics and the environment are well known, its impact on human sexuality is less well charted.

Ballard and *Crash*

James Graham Ballard was born in Shanghai, China, in 1930, where his father was a businessman. After the attack on Pearl Harbor, he and his family were interned in a civilian camp by the Japanese. The family returned to England in 1946. After two years at Cambridge, where he read medicine, Ballard began work as a copywriter, then as a Covent Garden porter before going to Canada with the RAF. His first short story was published in 1956, and at about the same time he took a full-time job on a technical journal. Later he became assistant editor on a scientific magazine where he stayed until 1961.

Ballard's first novel, *The Drowned World* (1962) was followed by *The Four Dimensional Nightmare* (1963), *The Terminal Beach* (1964), *The Drought* (1965) and *The Crystal World* (1966). These tales were brilliant, repetitive, highly original and obsessed by the adaptations needed to survive ecological disaster. Ballard created and re-created a series of startlingly vivid, loveless, dying, violent worlds. He came to occupy a respected niche in sci-fi.

Crash (1973) was turned down by several publishers and rumour has it that one reader's report said simply: 'this man is beyond psychiatric help'. *Crash* clearly followed on from Ballard's earlier work. It shows the car as an overwhelming natural disaster and explores its effect on human sexuality. Disconcertingly *Crash* does not suppose the end of the world: humanity survives the invention of the car, and then adapts to it – that is the problem. The point at which the car, instead of being shaped by humanity, has begun to shape humanity is one that has already gone by almost unnoticed. The book is a kind of auto-erotic dystopia.

In *Crash* Ballard is considering a condition akin to apotemnophilia, where the 'devotee' is sexually aroused by the sight, thought or proximity of amputees. But Ballard is also exploring the possibility that something like this rare fetish may in the future, through its close association with car crash injuries – particularly those involving famous people – become a part of general human sexuality. In the novel the crash victim/narrator meets Vaughan, a photographer who specializes in pictures of famous crash victims. The narrator is shown an album of Vaughan's pictures:

> The last group of photographs showed the young woman in a chromium wheelchair, guided by a friend across the rhododendron-screened lawn of a convalescent institution, propelling her shiny vehicle herself at an archery meeting, and finally taking her first lessons at the wheel of an invalid car. As she pondered the complex, treadle-operated brakes and gear changes I realized the extent to which this tragically injured young woman had been transformed during her recovery from the accident. The first photographs of her lying in the crashed car showed a conventional young woman whose symmetrical face and unstretched skin spelled out the whole economy of a cozy and passive life, of minor flirtations in the backs of cheap cars enjoyed without any sense of the real possibilities of her body. I could imagine her sitting in the car of some middle-aged welfare officer, unaware of the conjunction formed by their own genitalia and the stylized instrument panel, a Euclid of eroticism and fantasy that would

be revealed for the first time within the car-crash, a fierce marriage pivoting on the fleshy points of her knees and pubis. This agreeable young woman, with her pleasant sexual dreams, had been reborn within the breaking contours of her crushed sports car. Three months later, sitting beside her physiotherapy instructor in her new invalid car, she held the chromium treadles in her strong fingers as if they were extensions of her clitoris. Her knowing eyes seemed well aware that the space between her crippled legs was constantly within the gaze of this muscled young man. His eyes roved constantly among the damp moor of her pubis as she moved the gear lever through its cage. The crushed body of the sports car had turned her into a creature of free and perverse sexuality, releasing within its twisted bulkheads and leaking engine coolant all the deviant possibilities of her sex. Her crippled thighs and wasted calf muscles were models for fascinating perversities. As she peered through the window at Vaughan's camera her canny eyes were clearly aware of his real interest in her. The posture of her hands on the steering wheel and accelerator treadle, the unhealthy fingers pointing back towards her breasts, were elements in some stylized masturbatory rite. Her strong face with its unmatching planes seemed to mimic the deformed panels of the car, almost as if she consciously realized that these twisted instrument binnacles provided a readily accessible anthology of depraved acts, the keys to an alternative sexuality. I stared at the photographs in the harsh light. Without thinking, I visualized a series of imaginary pictures I might take of her: in various sexual acts, her legs supported by sections of complex machine tools, pulleys and trestles; with her physical education instructor, coaxing this conventional young man into the new parameters of her body, developing a sexual expertise that would be an exact analogue of the twentieth century. Thinking of the extensor rictus of her spine during orgasm, the erect hairs on her under muscled thighs, I stared at the stylized manufacturer's medallion visible in the photographs, the contoured flanks of the window pillars.

(Ballard 1973: 83)

Ballard's choice of subject and literary technique may be unorthodox, but intellectually he is the latest of several commentators to worry about the effect the car has had on humanity. Ballard successfully blends this with ideas on the pornography of violence. Where Ballard differs from his predecessors, is in the extremity and brutality of his vision.

Ballard's predecessors

H. G. Wells predicted the tank in his story 'The Land Ironclads', which appeared in *Strand* magazine in December 1903, more than fifteen years before the tank was actually invented. Wells anticipated the impact the tank would have on a battlefield still dominated by cavalry. Towards the end of the story a war journalist wonders about the new kind of man and the new mentality required to work these engines of war. For the first time in human history, killing has become mechanized and distant. The journalist notes one of the victors:

> He was a young man, healthy enough but by no means suntanned, and of a type of feature and expression that prevails in His Majesty's Navy: alert, intelligent, quiet. He and his engineers and riflemen all went about their work, calm and reasonable men. They had none of that flapping strenuousness of the half-wit in a hurry, that excessive strain upon the blood vessels, that hysteria of effort which is so frequently regarded as the proper state of mind for heroic deeds. [. . .] For the enemy these young engineers were defeating they felt a certain qualified pity and a quite unqualified contempt. They regarded these big, healthy men as they might regard some inferior kind of nigger. They despised them for making war; despised their bawling patriotisms and their emotionality profoundly; despised them, above all, for the petty cunning and the almost brutish want of imagination their method of fighting displayed. 'If they must make war,' these young men thought, 'why in thunder don't they do it like sensible men?' They resented the assumption that their own side was too stupid to do anything more than play their enemy's games, that they were going to play this costly folly according to the rules of unimaginative men. They resented being forced to the trouble of making man-killing machinery, resented the alternative of having to massacre these people or endure their truculent yappings; resented the whole unfathomable imbecility of war. Meanwhile, with something of the mechanical precision of a good clerk posting a ledger, the riflemen slowed their knobs and pressed buttons.
>
> (Wells 1977: 101–2)

Wells's point was that while people create technology, technology would inevitably work unpredictable changes in the human psyche.

The Italian poet Filippo Tomasso Marinetti began publishing around 1909 and later became a member of the Italian Fascist Party. He was profoundly influenced by the idea of technological advance and wrote manifestos on Futurism in *La Figaro*. He saw 'industrial war' as 'the world's only hygiene' and developed 'a machine aesthetic' in which he predicted that technology would alter the configuration of humanity. Marinetti predicted that a future machine-human would one day be constructed for 'omnipresent speed', and that it would be 'naturally cruel, omniscient, and aggressive'. He spoke of escaping one's boundaries and obtaining pleasure by means of 'violent, intoxicating acts', of the need for the exhilaration of speed, and the necessity of an armoured body, pointing out that machines were the expression but not the true purpose of humanity. For him 'the intoxication of great speed in cars was nothing but the joy of feeling oneself fused with the only divinity'. The struggle to make use of technology and still move towards some heroic non-mechanical destiny was the only real fight left for humanity.

Antonio Gramsci, the Italian revolutionary leader, wrote about 'Americanism and Fordism'. Gramsci lived in Turin, a city dominated by the Fiat company. Turin Fiat employed 30,000 workers and produced 90 per cent of all Italian vehicles at an average of seventy-five per day. Gramsci was one of the leaders of the great strike at Turin Fiat in 1920. He explored the changes a motorized society would work on the psyche of its inhabitants: he asked how the industrialization of Russia and the USA would impact on the inner lives of the workers. He was very clear that the car would raise the power of industry over the individual imagination and saw the car as the means of making workers pliable. Gramsci saw that life in industry demanded a process of 'psycho-physical' adaptation to the customs and conditions of industrial work. An important part of this was that the car, the thing the workers manufactured, became a symbol of working-class aspiration. This was a very neat self-perpetuating system (Spriano1975; Williams 1975).

Gramsci noted Ford's efforts to regulate the sexuality of the workers by enforcing marriage as the norm for employees. Gramsci was absolutely certain that the car would have a detrimental effect on human sexuality. He wanted a sexual revolution as part of a political revolution, and hoped a new society would redefine the ancient roles of 'man the hunter and woman the temptress' to enable the emergence of a whole new 'feminine' personality. When he listed how the car would affect humanity, item number two on the list was sex: 'a fundamental and autonomous aspect of the economic, and this sexual aspect raises, in its turn, complex problems' (Gramsci 1973: 295). He warned about the dangers of 'industry' tinkering with sexual mores for its own purposes:

> It is worth drawing attention to the way in which industrialists (Ford in particular) have been concerned with the sexual affairs of their employees and with their family arrangements in general. [. . .] The

truth is that the new type of man demanded by the rationalization of production and work cannot be developed until the sexual instinct has been suitably regulated and until it too has been rationalized.

(Gramsci 1973: 297)

'Fordism' could not control the direction of the changes it provoked. While it made the liberated sexuality of American workers dependent upon the prime symbol of industrial power and wealth – the motor car – at the same time it turned the car into an object of sexual desire. The motor car promised sexual liberation while it accomplished economic slavery. The car was an economic and sexual motor.

F. Scott Fitzgerald in *The Great Gatsby* (1926) made clear connections between his characters, their cars, the way they drove, their private lives and their sexuality. Gatsby's huge car, symbol of his wealth, his mystery and his attractiveness, stalks the novel like some mechanical penis:

> I'd seen it. Everybody had seen it. It was a rich cream color, bright with nickel, swollen here and there in its monstrous length with triumphant hat-boxes and supper-boxes and tool-boxes, and terraced with a labyrinth of wind-shields that mirrored a dozen suns.
>
> (Fitzgerald 2000 [1926]: 70)

In the 1930s the British literary magazine *Scrutiny* also addressed this theme. Denys Thompson wondered whether, instead of reinforcing the romance of 'high speed motoring', responsible intellectuals might not better serve the community by speculating as to 'how such joy affects the man who drives' (Thompson 1933: 187).

Ballard and Ralph Nader

An essential element to the development of Ballard's ideas on the car was the green-campaigner Ralph Nader, whose book *Unsafe at any Speed* (1971) attacked the advent of the motor car and emphasized the effect of the car on the human psyche. Nader had been writing about the US motor industry for several years and had built up a pressure group to lobby Washington with the intention of persuading Americans to rethink attitudes to 'their greatest dream image and totem object: the car'. Inevitably Nader clashed in the courts with General Motors, who saw him as a dangerous renegade intellectual, a critic of the American way of life and of the automobile industry – which in their eyes were one and the same. In the November 2000 presidential elections Nader decided to run on the green-consumer ticket. He polled a remarkable 3 per cent of the total vote.

Ballard has written enthusiastically about Nader on several occasions. When Ballard's book *The Atrocity Exhibition* (1969) was withdrawn from publication it was not because of its overripe language, nor for the piece entitled 'Why I want to fuck Ronald Reagan' (in which he predicted Reagan would become US President), but because Ballard showed his support for Nader and made clear the connection between the car and sex:

> The twentieth century has also given birth to a cast range of machines – computers, pilotless planes, thermonuclear weapons – where the latent identity of the machine is ambiguous even to the skilled investigator. An understanding of this identity can be found in a study of the automobile, which dominates the vectors of speed, aggression, violence and desire. In particular the automobile crash contains a crucial image of the machine as conceptualized psychopathology. Tests on a wide range of subjects indicate that the automobile, and in particular the automobile crash, provides a focus for the conceptualizing of a wide range of impulses involving the elements of psychopathology, sexuality and self sacrifice. [. . .] It is clear that the car crash is seen as a fertilizing rather than a destructive experience, a liberation of sexual and machine libido, mediating the sexuality of those who have died with an erotic intensity impossible in any other form.
>
> (Ballard 1969: 99)

Ballard summarized his feelings:

> We spend a large part of our lives in the car, and the experience of driving involves many of the experiences of being a human being in the 1970s, a focal point for an immense range of social, economic and psychological pressures. I think that the twentieth century reaches almost its purest expression on the highway. Here we see, all too clearly, the speed and violence of our age, its strange love affair with the machine and, conceivably, with its own death and destruction. What is the real significance in our lives of this huge metalized dream? Is the car, in more senses than one, taking us for a ride? Increasingly, the landscape of the twentieth century is being created by and for the car. [. . .] Sadly, despite the enormous benefits which the car has created, a sense of leisure, possibility, freedom and initiative undreamt of by the ordinary man eighty-six years ago when Karl Benz built the world's first petrol-driven vehicle, the car has brought with it a train of hazards and disasters, from the congestion of city and countryside to the serious injury and death of millions of people. The car crash is the most dramatic event in most people's lives apart from their own deaths,

and for many the two will coincide. Are we merely victims in a mean-ingless tragedy, or do these appalling accidents take place with some kind of unconscious collaboration on our part?

(Ballard 1996: 263)

The nature of Ballard's intervention

When *Crash* was reissued in 1995 Ballard wrote an introduction in which he clarified the nature of his intervention:

> *Crash* is [. . .] an extreme metaphor for an extreme situation, a kit of desperate measures only for use in an extreme crisis. *Crash*, of course, is not concerned with imagining disaster, however imminent, but with a pandemic cataclysm that kills hundreds of thousands of people each year and injures millions. Do we see, in the car crash, a sinister portent of a nightmare marriage between sex and technology? Well modern technology provides us with hitherto undreamed of means for tapping our own psychopathologies. Is this harnessing of our innate perversity conceivably of benefit to us? Is there some deviant logic unfolding more powerful than that provided by reason? Throughout *Crash* I have used the car not only as a sexual image but as a total metaphor for man's life in today's society. As such the novel has a political role quite apart from its sexual content, but I would still like to think that *Crash* is the first pornographic novel based on technology. In a sense pornography is the most political form of fiction, dealing with how we use and exploit each other in the most urgent and ruthless way.

(Ballard 1973: 6)

Angela Carter pointed out that in the 1970s and 1980s very few writers were dealing with the new circumstances and the dramatic social changes that had taken place since 1945. These writers, she said, saw themselves as 'beings in the world' because they had come to adult consciousness in the ruins of World War II and were the first generation to grow up 'with the reality of nuclear weapons' and the possibility of the end of the world (Carter 1998: 34). She also pointed out that what Ballard revealed was that the 'reality of British society seriously over stretched the traditional resources of British naturalistic fiction'. What Ballard craved, she wrote, was a revolutionary fiction that would both challenge and recognize the unconscious in a way that British fiction had never done before. What he wanted was, above all else, a fiction of the imagination that would some-how 'tell us the truth about ourselves':

Ballard became the great chronicler of the new, technological Britain. A man prone to thrust himself into the grip of obsession – 'I am my obsessions!' – he grew increasingly obsessed by aspects of our landscape those of us who grew up with the culturally programmed notion of Britain as a 'green and pleasant land' conspire to ignore. Motorways. High Rises. There eventually ensued novels of pure technological nightmare – *Crash*, *High Rise*, *The Concrete Island*. These were the vinyl and broken glass, sex 'n' violence novels, describing a landscape of desolation and disquiet similar to that of the novels of William Burroughs.

(Carter 1998: 560)

When he was interviewed about *Crash*, Ballard said that in the 1990s people were much more honest and open about their identities and the nature of their sexual interests, but this had not been the case when he was writing the book.

The idea that people could get any kind of excitement from the idea of car crashes – well people just couldn't cope with it, they thought it was totally insane. Now people are much more honest about the psychology of the late twentieth century and people can see, moreover, the way in which the car crash is built into the entertainment culture. No respectable Hollywood thriller has anything less than six car crashes. And people realize the extent to which aggression and libido are built into the experience of driving a car. [. . .] When people drive they have the possibility of death at their fingertips. And then, people are aware of a whole range of emotions that they can't express when they're in the office, that they can express alone in a car.

(http://www.reset.com/crash/cmp/ballard-interview)

Ballard and the new libido

With *Crash* Ballard presented something entirely new. He presented a vision of our world, of how we live, love, and how our libido is shaped. Shelley could have had Ballard in his visionary sights when he wrote, in 1821:

It is impossible to read the compositions of the most celebrated writers of the present day without being startled with the electric life that burns within their words. They measure the circumference and sound the depths of human nature with a comprehensive and all-penetrating spirit, and they are themselves perhaps the most sincerely astonished at its manifestations, for it is less their spirit than the spirit of the age.

Poets are the hierophants of an unapprehended inspiration, the mirrors of the gigantic shadows which futurity casts upon the present, the
words which express what they understand not; the trumpets which
sing to battle, and feel not what they inspire: the influence which is
moved not, but moves. Poets are the unacknowledged legislators of the
World.

(Shelley 1977: 508)

One of a writer's many responsibilities is to see what has never been seen
before, to say what has never been said and to predict where it is headed.
If the *auto* is now an adjunct to *amore*, if cars are an erotic stimulant and
what we are required to lust after, what we have been conditioned to love,
then why not make them objects of sexual lust in the way that film stars are
sex objects ('Blondes – Jayne Mansfield' 1999)?

The film of *Crash*

At its first showing at Cannes in May 1996, *Crash* ended to wild applause, a
standing ovation and loud booing. The jury awarded it a Special Jury Prize
for 'Originality, Daring and Audacity'. On 3 June 1996 Alexander Walker,
writing in *The London Evening Standard*, said the film featured 'some of
the most perverted acts and theories of sexual deviance I have ever seen
propagated in mainline cinema'. Another reviewer said it was 'pure pornography'. That autumn Fine Line Features, the video distribution company
handling *Crash*, got cold feet and tried to block the US release (Kadrey,
'*Crash* video lands on US'). The UK distributors were so uncertain of
the film's reception that they held a pre-screening press conference at
which the normally reclusive Ballard and the film's co-executive producer
appeared in an effort to dispel some of the mythology that had sprung up
around the film.

In November 1996 the film was granted a 'special certificate' in the UK
by the BBFC so that it could be screened at the London Film Festival. The
Daily Mail and the *London Evening Standard*, which ran the headline 'Beyond
the bounds of depravity', both campaigned to have it banned. Virginia
Bottomley, Government Heritage Secretary, called on local cinemas and
licensing authorities to ban the film, but only four councils did so. West-
minster Council, one of the four, went so far as to claim that the film
would 'deprave and corrupt'. In March 1997, after talks with the Home
Secretary, the BBFC decided that there was little actual violence in the
film, that an actress taking off her clothes inside a crashed vehicle in order
to engage in sex did not pose a threat to public morals, and that while the
film dealt with a form of sexual depravity it did not glorify or recommend

that depravity. The BBFC issued the film an '18' certificate and passed it uncut.

Cronenberg described UK press reaction as 'completely insane'. Ballard is reported to have been bemused and outraged by the press reaction: 'Half of America used to be conceived in the back of cars. There is nothing revolutionary in the idea that there is a sexual component to our idea of, or our excitement by, car crashes' (Hall, 'Future shock'). Neither the book nor the film is likely to bring about a sudden interest in car-crash sex. The point of both book and film is that when we make a fetish of the products and by-products of the car industry, a crossover from fact to fantasy, from one kind of lust to another, is inevitable. By partaking of the car and the injuries they cause we also share the possibility of fame, adoration and injury. Love me love my s/car. It is a perverse (perverted, even) version of Andy Warhol's notion of fifteen minutes of fame, but it is also a logical extension of the possibilities of the human psyche, a comment on the way we live, love and lust, on the way humans make and remake themselves.

9   Faking a life
Binjamin Wilkomirski, *Fragments*

This chapter deals with ideas of truth – autobiographical truth, psychological truth and historical truth. This chapter questions what happens when ideas about the truth of the writer's own story clash with the truth of a bigger historical picture, and when the writer's psychological needs contradict all the available evidence about their past. In particular this chapter makes a case study of Binjamin Wilkomirski's infamous *Fragments* and sets it against the background of Swiss identity problems and Holocaust denial.

This chapter asks: What is at stake when a writer invents not only a fake story of Holocaust survival, but also a fake personality and personal history to go with the story? What can we say when a writer's pain and anguish at their own past is so great that it overrides any and all sense of responsibility?

This chapter also revisits issues of accuracy, authenticity, identity and political context from earlier chapters.

Binjamin Wilkomirski's *Fragments: Memories of a Childhood 1939–1948* was first published in German in 1995 and caused an immediate sensation (Wilkomirski 1996). It purported to be one of the very rare records of a Jewish child from Latvia who survived Nazi genocide: its author claimed to have lived in both Majdanek and Auschwitz. Anna Karpf reviewed it at length in *The Guardian*, praising it as 'one of the great works about the Holocaust', and Katharine Viner ranked the book with works by Elie Wiesel, Anne Frank, Paul Celan and Claude Lanzmann (Karpf 1998: 2; Viner 1998: 2). It was very favourably reviewed by Maria Ross in the *Daily Mail*, Patricia Lee in the *Literary Review* and Paul Bailey in the *Daily Telegraph*. Holocaust historians hailed it as a masterpiece and it won the National Jewish Book Award in the USA, the *Jewish Quarterly* Literary Prize in the UK, and Le Prix de Mémoire de la Shoah in France. A favourable review of the book appeared in the specialist medical journal, *Medicine,*

Conflict and Survival (James 1999: 432). Since then it has been published in thirty countries and translated into sixteen languages, including Japanese. Wilkomirski toured the world relating his story, giving moving, tearful interviews, readings and performances, often to Holocaust survivors. He has also given lectures, appeared on TV in documentary films, and helped set up counselling for Holocaust survivors.

Doubts about authenticity

But not everyone was convinced. In February 1995 a Swiss journalist called Hanno Helbling contacted the German publishers to say that the author of the book was not Binjamin Wilkomirski, a Holocaust survivor. In August 1998 Swiss-Jewish writer Daniel Ganzfried, writing in *Die Welt-woche*, also began to voice doubts about the identity of the author and the authenticity of the book. Liepman AG, Wilkomirski's literary agents in Switzerland, engaged Dr Stefan Maechler to look into Wilkomirski's credentials and investigate the authenticity of the book (Maechler 2001). On the basis of Maechler's findings and her own research, Elena Lappin, editor of the *Jewish Quarterly*, wrote a long article voicing serious doubts about the book and the reliability of the author. This material was further supplemented by a BBC documentary (Ganzfried 1998; Gibbons and Moss 1999: 2; *Inside Story: Truth and Lies* 1999; Lappin 1999).

According to the best evidence available Wilkomirski was not Jewish, nor was he Latvian. He had never been a concentration camp inmate and had visited the camps only as an adult tourist. Latvian Jewish émigré camp survivor Binjamin Wilkomirski was in fact Swiss musician Bruno Grosjean, born on 12 February 1941, several years later than he claimed. His mother had been injured in a road accident and forced to give up her son for adoption: she had died in 1981. Records show that Bruno, aged three, was first fostered by Frau Aeberhard in a village near Nidau. This seems to have been a particularly difficult time for Bruno. Frau Aeberhard was a woman of unpredictable temper who seems to have kept him short of food and starved of affection. Later Bruno was taken to an orphanage in Adelboden. In the autumn of 1945 he was adopted by Dr and Mrs Dossekker. The couple were in late middle age and had no children of their own. Bruno lived in their comfortable home in the prosperous bourgeois district of Zurichberg in Zurich. Their relationship to Bruno seems to have been emotionally cool and physically distant, but in every sense supportive, responsible and caring.

As a result of their investigations the German publishers announced at the 1999 Frankfurt Book Fair that they had withdrawn *Fragments*. The Spanish and Swedish editions were cancelled. The English-language edition of the book, available in the USA, Canada, the UK and the Commonwealth had sold 32,800 copies and was quietly allowed to go out of print. Although the book had been well reviewed and had been a major literary event, it was not a commercial success. After four years the German, Italian and French editions combined had sold only 27,100 copies. As Maechler commented, no one made any real money from the book, even before the scandal: 'it was more a media event than a sales smash' (Maechler 2001: 119 and 333).

Questions of style

However, while the media fuss about the book has now died down, there are questions remaining about the veracity of the text of *Fragments*. There are questions about its peculiar and particular roots in Swiss experience. There is a general question as to why so many people were willing to believe the book and the author, and why so few realized it was fake? And there is a lingering and very awkward question as to what the fact of its fakeness means.

I had a very bad reaction to the book. It had been recommended to me by a friend, but after just a couple of pages something about it irritated me beyond measure: after ten pages I threw it at the wall. It was only with great reluctance that I was persuaded to finish reading it. It seemed to me that unlike the writings of Primo Levi, Bruno Bettelheim or Tadeusz Borowski, it traded on horror. Indeed the literary technique – the gaps, the improbability of the horrors, the child narrator, the 'must have been' mystery – seemed designed to take advantage of a kind of guilt and gullibility in the reader. It took advantage of a willingness to believe all the horrors, to say, yes it must have been so, even in response to sick invention. I thought the camps could make a person so sick they would enjoy recounting the horrors to a nice clean, comfortable, middle-class reader. For me the book was impressive, distasteful and possible. But it felt wrong. The main problem, and the main clue to the book's fakeness, is its style. The problem is present in the very first lines.

> I have no mother tongue, nor a father tongue either. My language has its roots in the Yiddish of my eldest brother Mordechai, overlaid with the Babel-babble of an assortment of children's barracks in the Nazis' death camps in Poland.
>
> It was a small vocabulary; it reduced itself to the bare essentials required to say and to understand whatever would ensure survival. At some point during this time, speech left me altogether and it was a long time before I found it again. So it was no great loss that I more

or less forgot this gibberish which lost its usefulness with the end of
the war.

(Wilkomirski 1996: 3)

This is a dramatic and emotional opening of which any novelist might be
proud. But as a personal record it leaves something to be desired. And it
runs counter not only to the rest of the book, but to the testimony of most
other camp survivors.

When did Wilkomirski lose his language? Language is crucial in any
account of concentration camp life. In most survivors acquisition of additional fragments of language, especially camp-German, enabled them to
work out what was going on, communicate and co-operate with other prisoners and survive a little longer. In this Wilkomirski directly contradicts
Auschwitz survivor Primo Levi:

> This not being talked to had rapid and devastating effects. To those
> who do not talk to you, or address you in screams that seem inarticu-
> late to you, you do not dare speak. If you are fortunate enough to
> have someone next to you with whom you have a language in
> common, good for you, you'll be able to exchange your impressions,
> seek counsel, let off steam, confide in him; if you don't find anyone
> your tongue dries up in a few days, and your thought with it. [. . .]
> The greater part of the prisoners who did not understand German –
> that is, almost all the Italians – died during the first ten to fifteen days
> after their arrival: at first sight, from hunger, cold, fatigue, and disease;
> but after a more attentive examination, due to insufficient information.
> If they had been able to communicate with their more experienced
> companions, they would have been able to orient themselves better:
> learn first of all to procure for themselves clothing, shoes, illegal food;
> avoid the harsher labor and the often lethal encounters with the SS;
> handle the inevitable illnesses without making fatal mistakes. I don't
> mean to say that they would not have died, but that they would have
> lived longer and had a greater chance of regaining lost ground.

(Levi 1988: 72)

If this was the case for an adult, surely it was even more so for a child. Had
Wilkomirski been unable to speak his already slim chances of survival
would have been reduced considerably. But if he ceased to speak, if he lost
the ability to understand language, then beyond this opening reference, it is
not mentioned or recorded in the remaining 154 pages of narrative.
Instead he recounts several conversations and repeatedly tells us not that
he is dumb, but that he is deaf, and then that he hears himself saying

things as if someone else said them (Wilkomirski 1996: 63). These are not the same things at all. However, given the other problems with this testimony, it is very revealing.

Narrative issues

The narrative of this book leaps about in time, making it very difficult to know exactly which years Wilkomirski is referring to. For example when he recounts events from his time in the orphanage we are never sure whether he is referring to the Polish orphanage at the end of the war, or to the Swiss orphanage after the war. This technique also makes it difficult to know whether we are to take every word as the testimony of a little boy, or whether, and to what extent, what we read has been filtered and rearranged by an adult. In a straightforward work of fiction these elements would make an intriguing challenge. But in a book subtitled *Memories of a Childhood 1939–1948*, they are disconcerting, even misleading.

On certain key issues of fact Wilkomirski is vague. Very early in the book he tells us: 'It must have been Riga, in winter' (Wilkomirski 1996: 6). It is interesting if it is Riga, since this is a real place with a real history. It is an anchor of sorts for a child's story that has very few links to adult reality. It is certainly convenient for Wilkomirski that we accept the idea that it must be Riga. But *must* it be Riga? Why? We never find out why. But clearly if it might be Riga the reader would like to know what the other possibilities are, whereas, if it must be Riga the author has already sifted the other possibilities and presented us with his conclusion. It must be Riga for no other reason than that the author says so. In Riga he watches the death of a man. 'Maybe my father', he says. And then goes on: 'All at once I realize: From now on I will have to manage without him' (Wilkomirski 1996: 6). This is confusing. If this is the boy's father why does the child not know this? Does he have no emotional link to the man? He can see the man is hurt, even if he has no idea of death. And if this is not his father, why will he have to manage without him?

The text often works this way – edging from a question to the emotional content of a certainty, without ever making the connection absolutely clear. The technique allows Wilkomirski both to have a father and to be alone, to have lost a father and not to have the emotional bother of having to give him a character or to mourn him. It allows Wilkomirski the odd gift of accruing all the emotional sympathy we might give a child who has witnessed the death of his father, without the difficulty of having to sketch in a relationship with that father, or the emotional burden of having to mourn for his loss. Wilkomirski has it both ways by simultaneously having and not having a father. Indeed Wilkomirski's sense of being alone, even when he is surrounded by others – brothers, prisoners, friends, health workers – is steady throughout the book.

The confusion over shifts in time allows Wilkomirski to play upon the reader's emotions. In his depiction of life in both the Polish and Swiss orphanages we are led to believe that this child has never seen jam, does not accept bread from anyone except his mother, that he thinks the Swiss basement laundry is reminiscent of camp bunk-beds, and finds that the central heating boiler reminds him of the furnaces at the camp – which, if he ever saw, he did not tell us about. For the most part he can get away with these things by claiming that these are the memories of a child, and that he could not reasonably be expected to recount his story or to 'know' facts in the way an adult might.

But Wilkomirski trades on the gullibility of the reader, the willingness to believe all horrors. He has the reader for a willing fool. He claims that when they were not allowed out of their huts they would use the area between the bunks as a toilet. In order to keep his feet warm, he says, and on advice given by his friend Jankl, he stood up to his ankles in excrement (Wilkomirski 1996: 59). Here there is clearly a general point to be made about dwelling on such horrors. There is another point to be made about the likelihood of such a thing. And there is the question of practicality. Excrement freezes, just like everything else. People on a starvation diet of watery soup pass liquid, not solid excrement. To say that this is unscrupulous play with the reader's willing belief and sympathetic emotion is an understatement. This is a kind of obscenity.

Swiss identity

Though the Swiss literary establishment has been reluctant to acknowledge the scandal, and slow to identify correspondences, it is no accident that Wilkomirski's *Fragments* has the author transpose a fairly well documented and clearly unhappy childhood in an orphanage, and then as an adopted child in Zurich, into the brutal tale of his life as a Holocaust survivor. Bruno Grosjean, while he was not Jewish and was certainly not a concentration camp survivor, was another kind of 'outsider' to legitimate Swiss identity. Bruno Grosjean was the illegitimate son of a mother who was a Swiss *verdingkind* – an earning child. It is difficult to grasp the depth of shame this implies in Switzerland.

The system of *verdingkinder* began some time in the 1800s. It was designed to reduce the burden to the communes of maintaining the poor by simply taking their children away from them. It seems that the first (and virtually the only) time anyone troubled to consider the fate of these children was in 1837, when Berne writer Jeremias Gotthelf wrote a comprehensive survey called *Bauernspiegel* (Mirror of Farmers: A Reflection on Poverty among the Peasant Classes). Gotthelf revealed that the communes were auctioning poor children in a manner reminiscent of American slave markets, except that in Switzerland the bid went to the person who put in the lowest figure for the child's upkeep. These children were in great demand, not because farmers wanted to give them a better life, but simply because they were cheap labour (Waidson 1978). Meticulous local government ledgers record that children were sold for as little as 10 Swiss francs per year – about a quarter of what the average farmer made per week by taking produce to market. Most of these children worked the land, though some were placed in factory workshops. They were usually treated badly and often malnourished because at the table (if they ever got that far) they were placed 'furthest from the pot'; only very rarely were these children given any kind of an education, and they were never offered payment for their labour. They were slaves in all but name. Only in the 1870s was federal regulation introduced to control the sale, but not the treatment, of *verdingkinder*. By 1910 there were still over 10,000 *verdingkinder* in Berne canton alone.

Gradually, federal regulation forced the communes to abandon the auction system, to appoint inspectors and to monitor 'foster' homes, but the system still left children open to abuse and remained a kind of official slave market. A campaign to abolish the *verdingkinder* system was launched in 1945. By 1955 the state claimed that the whole system, which by now was uneconomical, had gone. However, rumours persist to this day that 'earning children' are still to be found in rural districts. Possibly the rumours are just a guilty memory of the child slave market and the lingering, peculiarly Swiss sense of shame and stigma attached to lack of wealth (Saunders 2000: 14).

While Bruno Grosjean may have metamorphosed himself into something he is not, it is clear that he translated Swiss-German unease over legitimacy, identity and fears of a hidden Swiss social reality by writing the content of his young life in Switzerland as an echo of life under the Nazis. His childhood, he is saying, was a kind of Shoah, a destruction of his real past, an attempt to remake him as a good little Swiss, an emotional Holocaust. He could not be a good Swiss, that much is clear, simply because he is unhappy with the person he finds himself to be, and he has made a desperate bid to be a different 'self' by explaining his unhappiness in a particular way. But the literary self he has chosen is perhaps not so very far from the self he might have been: he is, after all, the illegitimate son of a woman who represented the embarrassing, unreliable, poor underclass of *verdingkinder*, a category of humanity the Swiss had tried to make both profitable and invisible.

There is a direct connection between the history of *verdingkinder* and

Fragments, and it comes through the very modern questions of authenticity, identity, citizenship and our relation to the state. We all feel these things and we all have calls made upon us by the state, by distant relatives and residual identities. But in Switzerland these things are felt in a way that most Europeans do not experience since Switzerland's democracy obscures a history of and a host of social traits and economic links to Nazism. For example, it has become clear since the late 1980s that Switzerland was Hitler's main accomplice and the sole direct beneficiary of Nazi war plunder. Switzerland's spectacular rise from prewar rural poverty to postwar wealth and economic security can only be explained by its processing of Nazi plunder through the banks. An act such as this is linked, invisibly, inevitably and inextricably, to the kind of place Switzerland is.

Switzerland's record in dealing with Gypsies, Jews and other refugees during the war, and 'guest workers' after the war, leaves much to be desired (Berger 1975). Switzerland rejected votes for women in 1959, allowed them to vote in national elections only in 1971, and did not allow women to vote in cantonal elections until the 1980s (but in the Appenzell canton women could not vote until 1990). In Switzerland repression takes place in the area of identity and loyalty. Sex, money, poverty, crime, immigration, housing, marriage are adjuncts to this. These are areas of Swiss social-identity crime. In Switzerland failure to conform is un-Swiss, un-bourgeois. Switzerland is a state with an overpowering and claustrophobic interest in social, national and ethnic homogeneity, in policing identity, and bourgeois Swiss society does this not only through the usual social pressures (backed up by bureaucracy and where necessary by riot police), but through the use of imported foreign labour, by concealing and controlling racism rather than confronting it, through rigorously controlling access to citizenship, through the power of the market, by tying the quality of life to the nature of Swiss-ness, and by denying the financial origins and roots of its postwar identity and wealth.

It is no accident that Switzerland has been so reluctant to join the EU. The EU threatens Swiss-ness in ways that outsiders can hardly begin to grasp, simply because it demands a sense of the world and an integrity that overrides Swiss-ness, insists on a wider perspective than Swiss-ness, and posits a measure of humanity that overrides the preservation of local identity, the unanimity of the commune, the financial probity and ethnic purity of approved identity. At almost the same time *Fragments* was published, George Steiner (who spent several years in Switzerland) pointed to the word *frontalier*, 'the grim Swiss word for those who, materially and psychologically, dwell near or astride borders', and he asked readers to ponder the implications of the existence of this word and this mentality for literature and identity (Steiner 1996: 148). Steiner's comment was prescient. In many ways *Fragments* is an example of the achievement of this mentality. In *Fragments* the cruelties, pain, desire, the longing to belong are all expressions of otherness, aloneness, apartness, unconformity, unease at privilege, desire to be different, desire to name and shame those who caused pain, a desire to be legitimate, a potent desire to be someone else.

Suffering and eroticism

In *Fragments* part of the reaction to this mentality is the author's enjoyment of suffering and a lingering charnel house eroticism aimed directly at bourgeois Swiss sensibilities:

> On their way to the latrines they hadn't been able to hold their water anymore. Two of the block wardens had caught them as they were peeing against the wall behind one of the barracks. As a punishment, they'd taken little sticks and pushed them up into the boys' penises as far as they'd go. Then the block wardens had hit their penises, making the sticks break off. The wardens had laughed a lot and had a good time.
>   'Now all they'll do is pee blood,' said one of them.
>
> (Wilkomirski 1996: 60)

These events have the feeling of a sadomasochistic fantasy rather than an actual event. It must be said that most men would be reluctant to handle a penis that is not their own. The idea of touching a child's penis is almost unthinkable – even a brutal sadist would be more inclined to hit the child. And how, practically, are we to understand that this was done? Did one man hold the child? If the incident took place it would take three, perhaps four people to do such a thing. Did they do it to both boys? Why did not the second child run away? The author enjoys the idea of the horrors too much and he has no details to offer. He is too keen to shock us, to make us suffer for his suffering. But this incident also casts doubt on the scene where Wilkomirski claims to have stood in excrement in order to keep warm. If we are to believe what happens to the children for daring to relieve themselves in the wrong place, how likely is it that people would relieve themselves inside the barracks? The incident is constructed to offend bourgeois sensibilities.

In a further incident two babies are deposited in a prison hut overnight. We learn that: 'Frozen fingers don't hurt', and that 'Sometime in the night they chewed their fingers down to the bone' (Wilkomirski 1996: 71). Again we have to ask: is this likely? Isn't it more likely these children would have been killed immediately on arrival at the camp, during selection? They may somehow have survived the selection process, perhaps destined for some medical experiment, but even then, is it likely that they would have eaten their own hands? Did they have the teeth for this? Both hands? Both children? Overnight? And then died? The enjoyment of the invented horrors goes hand in hand with the desire to punish everyone else for his unhappiness by rubbing noses in these imagined horrors. Wilkomirski's 'concentration camp kitsch' is shocking, but not necessarily for the reasons he supposes.

The idea of kitsch connects the book to the violent excess and joy in horror shown in the charnel house imagery of the later Jacobean dramatists. Their fascination with images of horror came about mainly because of the shocking contrast between the awakened individual mind and the frustration of expectations awaiting that mind in the real world. Later, in the eighteenth century, the horrors of the Gothic novel came about through frustration resulting from the massive political, scientific and aesthetic awakening of that period, and the clash with the horrors of the French Revolution and the Napoleonic wars. The literary discovery made in different ways by both Renaissance and Enlightenment writers was that horror could be a source of delight, 'the Horrid' could be a category of beauty, and pain could be part of desire. In *Idée sur les romans* (written sometime before 1800), De Sade said:

> This genre was the inevitable product of the revolutionary shocks with which the whole of Europe resounded. For those who were acquainted with all the ills that are brought upon men by the wicked, the romantic novel was becoming somewhat difficult to write, and merely monotonous to read: there was nobody left who had not experienced more misfortunes in four or five years than could be depicted in a century by literature's most famous novelists: it was necessary to call upon hell for aid in order to arouse interest, and to find in the land of fantasies what was common knowledge from historical observation of man in this iron age. But this way of writing presented so many inconveniences.
>
> (Praz 1968: 10)

For example, in M. G. Lewis's novel *The Monk* (1796), Agnes is condemned to a long slow death with her unborn child, in a dungeon. After she has given birth we have the following passage:

> Sometimes I felt the bloated toad, hideous and pampered with the poisonous vapors of the dungeon, dragging its loathsome length along my bosom. Sometimes the quick cold lizard roused me, leaving its slimy

track upon my face and entangling itself in the tresses of my wild and matted hair. Often have I at wakening found my fingers ringed with the long worms which bred in the corrupted flesh of my infant.

(Praz 1968: 10)

The shock of enjoyment in these horrors is clear. This 'horrible unreality', as De Sade called it, is not so very far from *Fragments*.

In some ways *Fragments* is also a perverse echo of Mary Shelley's *Frankenstein* (1818). There too, in an alpine Swiss setting, there is an attempt to make a new man from unsatisfactory fragments. In the late twentieth century the fragments are different from those available in the late eighteenth century, but the result is still a broken kind of monster, a parody of the real victim, a parody of the actual event. But that is not the end of the matter, since, as in Mary Shelley's novel, the parody reveals things to us, not only about itself, but about the thing it seeks to parody and the thing it seeks to be a part of.

History, because it is past, can only ever be perceived as it is presented. Wilkomirski is not the first to employ fake horror as a literary technique to deal with World War II. William Styron's *Sophie's Choice* (1979) and Jerzy Kosinski's *The Painted Bird* (1965) are other examples of the phenomenon. There is no doubt that these are books of nightmare. The question is whether we accept them as accurate portrayals of historical events given personal dimensions through the novel form, or whether we say they are in themselves a kind of late Gothic fiction, the products of the tortured imaginations of very unhappy writers. However, there is more to this than Wilkomirski's personal needs, and more to writing than historical ambulance chasing. By producing a fake personality to go with the memoir, Wilkomirski pointed up the unreliability of oral and personal testimony in an area where a great many documents are missing and where there are enormous voids in our understanding of the Holocaust and the people who enabled it. He underlined just how fragile are the achievements of oral history and autobiography in the face of the Holocaust, and emphasized that the distinction sometimes made between literary imagination and memoir is not clear. Worse, Wilkomirski has brought into question the personality and reliability of survivors. Worse still, he has made survivors seem like people with a psychological disorder, rather than people struggling to make sense of an experience that defies description or explanation.

Historical truth

Fragments appeared against a backdrop of political shifts and intellectual difficulties which included reaction to the collapse of communism, a general rightward move in political opinion throughout Europe, a resurgence of extreme right-wing opinion and a rise in neo-Nazi political activity and a steady resurgence of intolerance, xenophobia and anti-Semitism. Paul de Man's influential post-modernist literary theories were discovered to have their roots in his silence about his complicity with Nazism in wartime Belgium; David Irving was suing Deborah Lipstadt for daring to call him a Holocaust denier; Jewish organizations were trying to oust Catholic shrines from Auschwitz; debates about the historical 'truth' of Claud Lanzmann's *Shoah*, a filmed oral record of anti-Semitism, and Steven Spielberg's *The Last Days*, a massive filmed oral history of the Holocaust with sufficient testimony to run continuously for fifty years, were developing. Perhaps more importantly, Wilkomirski's book appeared at a time when Switzerland was reassessing its wartime connection and its postwar debt to Nazism. This was an atmosphere in which any memoir of the Holocaust revealed to be false played into the hands of neo-Nazi Holocaust deniers and in which World War II and the Holocaust were in the public domain in a way they had never been before (Lehman 1991; Lipstadt 1993; Evans 1997; Lee 1997).

Wilkomirski has not given us a portrait of his experiences as a child of the Holocaust. He has given us a picture of the emotional world he inhabited as the illegitimate son of a social outcast in Switzerland. The equivalence in his mind is clear. It is some bizarre Swiss Holocaust of the soul. By the time this child arrived at the Dossekker home he already had a daunting and depressing past. It was of this he needed to speak. There can be no doubt that his writing has power and skill and is packed with emotion. But as it stands, for purely personal needs he has unwittingly undermined the fact of the Holocaust, and by drawing attention to his own unreliability as a 'witness' he has made other witnesses less credible. He may have gone some way to salving his personal problems by expressing himself in this way, and may have embarrassed the Swiss in the process, but he has also offered ammunition to Holocaust deniers.

Fragments also circles uneasily round the problem of the pornography of violence and the difficulty of charting just what the human psyche is capable of. But it also brings into question the possibility of autobiographical and historical 'truth'. Wilkomirski, in surrendering to the satisfaction of his own personal needs, exposed his lack of control over the form in which he chose to write, his failure to imagine how the book would be received. Clearly he was deeply uncertain as to what exactly he wanted to accomplish and lacked any awareness of the dangers in faking a Holocaust memoir. However, he did this at the very moment when the Holocaust itself had become a historical and philosophical 'issue'. The timing of these two things makes it difficult, but we have to wonder what the Holocaust and the Nazis have come to mean. Do we now accept every fictional invention about them? Are they now no more than a kind of literary lightning-rod for outlandish imaginings and sadomasochistic writing?

It has been said that *Fragments* is the product of psychological therapy the author undertook for depression, that it is a case of 'recovered false memory', and that the real fault lies with the therapy itself (html://www. stopbadtherapy.com/experts/fragments/fragments). This may be so: but it does not alter the fact that the book is a banal sadomasochistic fantasy masquerading as an authentic and very rare autobiography. Almost all of those who once honoured Wilkomirski have now withdrawn the awards they presented. In Zurich a magistrate even investigated whether charges of fraud should be brought against the author.

10 Sex, satire and sadism

Bret Easton Ellis, *American Psycho*

The following chapter makes a case study of *American Psycho*, a highly controversial attempt to satirize yuppie culture on Wall Street in the 1980s. More
than a decade has passed since the book was published but the questions and
doubts about it persist.

Perhaps the book is telling us something important but unpleasant about
the way we live and the way the world really works. But if so, does the satire
encourage or discourage the behaviour it exposes? Is it really a textbook on
how to humiliate and murder women? Are the killings of men just a ploy to
make it look even-handed? Is there a deeply misogynist element at work? Do
the satire and the comedy outweigh the sex and violence?

This chapter also revisits issues of political correctness, originality and
censorship.

The background

Bret Easton Ellis was born in Los Angeles in 1964. His first novel *Less Than
Zero* (1985) was already a bestseller by the time he graduated from Bennington College and it made him very wealthy:

> I made an enormous amount of money and I moved to Manhattan
> and I sort of got sucked up into this whole yuppie-mania that was
> going on at that time and I think in a lot of ways, working on *American
> Psycho* was my way of fighting against slipping into a certain kind of
> lifestyle. [. . .] And so when I moved here, I started meeting a lot of
> young guys who were working on Wall St and I thought, great, here's
> the perfect takeoff point for what I want to do; it's about money, it's
> about hollow money, it's about how can these kids be making these
> enormous sums of money during this time. [. . .] I knew a lot of friends

at Bennington whose brothers were making a fortune on Wall St and just living the whole 80's life and so I hung out with these guys for about two weeks because I wanted to find out what exactly people were doing. Now of course we know they're in jail, and so I know now why they couldn't talk about certain things, why they didn't take me to their offices, why they weren't extremely clear cut about what exactly their jobs entailed, how they were making so much money, etc. [. . .] At the end of the day, it was always meet at Harry's, meet the new bimbo they're dating, what's the hippest restaurant, talk about buying a car, talk about houses in the Hamptons they wanted to rent, which club they go to, where their dealer was, buying suits, clothes, trips, etc. So after two exhausting weeks of hanging out with these people, I understood that my narrator would be a serial killer. I don't know where I made the connection; it just seemed logical that one of these guys would be driven so nuts by how status obsessed everyone is, that it would incite him into becoming a murderer.

(Clarke 1996/98)

Ellis was paid an advance of $300,000: he began *American Psycho* in December 1986 and finished it in November 1989. He had discussed the manuscript with his agent and with his editor at Simon and Schuster. Neither of them thought it was likely to prove a commercial success, which is a surprise, given the size of his advance, but perhaps the size of the advance was a symptom of the very subject Ellis had chosen to write about. If anything, his agent and editor were worried about the book:

I mean, where's the detective? I mean where's the girl in danger? Why isn't he caught in the end? What's going on here? What are all these clothes? What is going on? You've got to cut all this out, the book is like 200 pages too long!

(Lawson n.d.)

At this stage nobody seems to have objected to the violence or misogyny. However in the autumn of 1990, just four weeks before it was due for distribution to bookshops, information was leaked to the press that the publisher had decided not to go ahead with publication. The rumour was that in-house editors found the book so offensive and misogynistic they simply refused to work on it. Ellis has always claimed that the book is about 'a larger metaphor – alienation, pain, America, the overall tone of the culture' (Clarke 1996/98).

Almost immediately Vintage agreed to pick up the book and just prior to publication extracts appeared in *Time* and *Spy* magazines. It was at once clear what the fuss had been about. In one of the extracts a woman was skinned alive and in the other a victim's head was removed and then used for sex by the killer. When the book itself appeared this impression was confirmed.

Yuppies in New York

The story concerns a young, very successful man called Patrick Bateman. He is a Wall Street dealer of some sort – we never find out exactly what he does. Bateman is also a psychopathic killer. He commits at least fourteen killings in the book, including a five-year-old child, and he refers to other attacks and killings we do not witness. The victims are men and women, but the women definitely die much more painfully and slowly than the men. He also kills or wounds several dogs.

Ellis at first dismissed all criticism as mere worry that he had committed 'defamation of clothing'. However, as he began to receive hate mail and death threats he was forced to reconsider not just the fashion element of the work, but the violence – particularly against women:

> It actually did come on suddenly. There were a lot of warning signs if I look back on it. But when the publisher decided he wouldn't publish the book, that came very suddenly. I knew there was a lot of pre-controversy and there were problems in-house and the guy who did my covers before backed away saying it was the most disgusting thing he'd ever read, blahblahblah. [. . .] I was totally, totally shocked. [. . .] This was the last thing in the world I thought would've happened. I thought maybe they would publish the book and maybe people would be upset by it, I guess, but I never thought they would not publish the book and I never thought that, for example, the National Organization for Women would call for a boycott of the book, or the book would cause this kind of fury. I just didn't think this was going to happen. I didn't think there was enough in the book to make it that shocking.
>
> (Clarke 1996/98)

At first the gruesome nature of the killings, the lingering descriptions of torture and death agonies and the narrator's misogyny dominated the way the book was received, but gradually another reading, where these things are not the focus but merely a part of a much bigger story, has become possible. We can now see the book very clearly as a satire on the coke-fuelled hedonistic money culture – on both sides of the Atlantic – of the Reagan–Thatcher years. Ellis says that New York had always inspired him and that he had long wanted to set a book there. Ellis has said that: 'New York is a pretty good guide for what's going on in terms of the times and what's going on or going to go on with the rest of the country' (Clarke 1996/98). At the very start of the book yuppie Timothy says:

> 'I hate to complain – I really do – about the trash, the garbage, the disease, about how filthy this city really is and *you* know and I know it is a *sty* . . . ' He [. . .] pulls out today's newspaper. 'In one issue – in *one* issue – let's see here . . . Strangled models, babies thrown from tenement rooftops, kids killed in the subway, a Communist rally, Mafia boss wiped out, Nazis [. . .] baseball players with AIDS, more Mafia shit, gridlock, the homeless, various maniacs, faggots dropping like flies in the streets, surrogate mothers, the cancellation of a soap opera, kids who broke into a zoo and tortured and burned various animals alive, more Nazis . . . and the joke is, the punch line is, it's all in this city – nowhere else, just here, it sucks, whoa wait, more Nazis, gridlock, gridlock, baby-sellers, black-market babies, AIDS babies, baby junkies, building collapses on baby, maniac baby, gridlock, bridge collapses.'
>
> (Ellis 1991: 4)

Bateman has no compassion, no mercy, no insight into what his job entails or into himself. Like his other yuppie friends he believes that his efforts are not adequately rewarded and that he should be earning more money. As yuppie Price says, on the very first page of the novel: 'I'm resourceful, I'm creative, I'm young, unscrupulous, highly motivated, highly skilled. In essence what I'm saying is that society can*not* afford to lose me. I'm an *asset*' (Ellis 1991: 3). Bateman is obsessed with power, financial and physical. He spends a great deal of his time toning his body. He frequently attends the gymnasium, delights in talking about his personal trainer and details endlessly how many 'reps' of his weightlifting exercises he can do (Ellis 1991: 69). He is obsessed by the latest fashion in restaurants, music and shows. He is obsessed by designer clothing, deodorants, skin care products and furniture: he gives us a seven-page-long, detailed description of his bedroom, his bathroom and his morning grooming habits, complete with product details (Ellis 1991: 24). This is a vapid world of conspicuous consumption and endless conversation about where to eat and what to buy next:

> J&B I am thinking. Glass of J&B in my right hand I am thinking. Jami Gertz I am thinking. I would like to fuck Jami Gertz I am thinking. Porsche 911. A sharpie I am thinking. I would like to own a sharpie. I

am twenty six years old I am thinking. I will be twenty seven next year. A Valium. I would like a Valium. No, *two* Valium I am thinking. Cellular phone I am thinking.

(Ellis 1991: 81)

For Bateman, perhaps, this is thinking.

The yuppies constantly eye each other's clothing: there are long descriptions of clothes and long discussions of how to match and wear accessories. Bateman, for example, observes one of his associates: 'He takes off his glasses (Oliver Peoples, of course) and yawns, wiping them clean with an Armani handkerchief' (Ellis 1991: 35). A little later Bateman wears a pair of the same spectacles – though his have plain glass rather than corrective lenses. Bateman even keeps his 'Nike all sport sneakers' on while having sex (Ellis 1991: 173).

Bateman is also obsessed with exclusive and expensive restaurants and bothered by where his table is positioned as if this reflects his status. He is obsessed with what he eats and drinks, not that he has a genuine interest in food, but because it gives him an opportunity to wave around his Platinum Am Ex credit card:

> We're seated at a mediocre table near the back section of the main dining room. [. . .] For dinner I order the shad-roe ravioli with apple compote as an appetizer and the meat loaf with chèvre and quail-stock sauce for an entrée. She orders the red snapper with violets and pine nuts and for an appetizer a peanut butter soup with smoked duck and mashed squash which sounds strange but is actually quite good. *New York* magazine called it a 'playful but mysterious little dish' and I repeat this to Patricia.
>
> (Ellis 1991: 77)

Bateman cannot grasp that other people do not share his view of the world or his system of values and is baffled when his colleague Luis describes taking to dinner two out of town clients – 'total *hicks*':

> 'What did you order?' I ask.
> 'I had the poached oysters, the lotte and the walnut tart.'
> 'I hear the lotte is good there,' I murmur, lost in thought.
> 'The client had the boudin blanc, the roast chicken and the cheesecake,' he says.
> 'Cheesecake?' I say, confused by this plain, alien sounding list. 'What sauce or fruits were on the roasted chicken? What shape was it cut into?'
> 'None, Patrick,' he says, also confused. 'It was . . . roasted.'

'And the cheesecake, what flavor? Was it heated?' I say. 'Ricotta cheesecake? Goat cheese? Were there flowers or cilantro in it?'

'It was just . . . Regular,' he says, and then, 'Patrick, you're sweating.'

'What did she have?' I ask, ignoring him. 'The client's bimbo.'

'Well, she had the country salad, the scallops and the lemon tart,' says Luis.

'The scallops were grilled? Were they sashimi scallops? In a ceviche of sorts?' I'm asking. 'Or were they *gratinized*?'

'No, Patrick,' Luis says. 'They were . . . broiled.'

It's silent in the boardroom as I contemplate this, thinking it through before asking, finally, 'What's "broiled", Luis?'

'I'm not sure,' he says. 'I think it involves . . . a pan.'

(Ellis 1991: 107)

Bateman's knowledge of music is as comprehensive as his understanding of cookery. He gives us three whole chapters analysing Whitney Houston, Genesis and Huey Lewis and the News. He is knowledgeable up to a point, and mistakenly believes Phil Collins wrote 'A Groovy Kind of Love' (Ellis 1991: 101). His choice of music proves only that his taste is bland, vapid, middle of the road and unadventurous. If anything his interest in these particular 'artists' and the way he writes about them point up the extent to which these are transparent products of the entertainment world, pop acts designed simply to make money by appealing to the widest possible fan base by being bland and inoffensive.

Bateman, though he prides himself on his knowledge of yuppie etiquette, is not as clever as he likes to pretend. At one point Bateman in a drug haze blunders into a Kosher restaurant and asks for a milk shake and a '*kosher*-burger but *with cheese*' (Ellis 1991: 152). And even among yuppies, he is not a great success. His colleagues frequently comment sarcastically on his permanent suntan. He shows off his newly designed business card, only for three colleagues to pull out better-quality cards while his 'lies on the table, ignored': he admits he is 'unexpectedly depressed' that he showed his card at all (Ellis 1991: 44).

Yuppies and women

None of the things Bateman buys gives him any pleasure though. His obsessions are just demonstrations of financial power. In a conversation about how to behave with women, one of Bateman's colleagues says:

'Like these girls *care*,' Price snorts. 'When I tell them what my annual income is, believe me, my behavior couldn't matter less.'

'And how do you drop this little tidbit of info?' Van Patten asks. 'Do you say, Here's a Corona and by the way I pull in a hundred eighty thou a year and what's your sign?'

'One ninety,' Price corrects him, and then, 'Yeah, I do. Subtlety is not what these girls are after.'

(Ellis 1991: 53)

Bateman behaves much the same as Price.

'Don't you want to know what I do?'

The two of them stare at me for a long time. Fixed smiles locked on their faces, they glance at each other before Christie, unsure, shrugs and quietly answers, 'No'.

Sabrina smiles, takes this as a cue and agrees. 'No, not really.'

I stare at the two of them for a minute before re-crossing my legs and sighing, very irritated. 'Well I work on Wall Street. At Pierce & Pierce.'

(Ellis 1991: 171)

Young women are 'bimbos' 'hardbodies' or 'total hardbodies'. They are not intellectuals, they are barely even people:

If they have a good personality then . . . something is very wrong. [. . .] There are no girls with good personalities. A good personality consists of a chick who has a little hardbody and who will satisfy all sexual demands without being too slutty about things and who will essentially keep her dumb fucking mouth *shut*.

(Ellis 1991: 91)

Their purpose in life is to be available for expensive sex: like everything else, whether they are the call-girls and prostitutes Bateman uses, the girls he knows from work, his fiancée or the girls he dates, they are simply commodities to be bought and sold. As Bateman says of Courtney:

If she likes me only for my muscles, the heft of my cock, then she's a shallow bitch. *But* a physically superior, near perfect-looking shallow bitch, and *that* can override anything, except maybe bad breath or yellow teeth, either of these is a real deal-breaker.

(Ellis 1991: 157)

Yuppie women

The women in the book, while they are all in their own ways as obsessed as
the men, and totally unprepared for an encounter with a psychopath, are
at least as intelligent as the men – but that is not saying much. The conversation of the yuppie women is as uninspirational and consumer oriented as
that of the male yuppies. They certainly do not have the respect of the
male yuppies:

> 'I need a new fur,' Libby sighs, staring into her champagne glass.
> 'Full length or ankle length?' Daisy asks in the same toneless voice.
> 'A stole?' Caron suggests.
> 'Either a full length or . . . ' Libby stops and thinks hard for a
> minute. 'I saw this short, cuddly wrap . . . '
> 'But mink, right?' Daisy asks. 'Definitely *mink?*'
> 'Oh yeah. Mink,' Libby says.
> 'Hey Taylor,' I whisper, nudging him. 'Wake up. They're talking.
> You gotta see this.'
> 'But *which* kind?' Caron's on a roll.
> 'Don't you find some minks are too . . . *fluffy?*' Daisy asks.
> 'Some minks *are* too fluffy.' Libby this time.
> 'Silver fox is *very* popular,' Daisy murmurs.
> 'Beige tones are also increasingly popular.' Libby says.
> 'Which ones are those?' someone asks.
> 'Lynx. Chinchilla. Ermine. Beaver – '
> 'Silver fox is very popular,' one of them says.
> 'Raccoon. Fitch. Squirrel. Muskrat. Mongolian lamb.'
> 'Am I dreaming,' Taylor asks me, 'or . . . am I really hearing an
> actual conversation?'
> 'Well, I suppose what passes for one.' I wince. 'Shhh. Listen. It's
> inspiring.'
>
> (Ellis 1991: 203)

The satire is relentless; the detail is endless, vacuity fathomless. But yuppie
male conversation is as inane as that of yuppie women:

> There's this theory out now that if you can catch the AIDS virus
> through having *sex* with someone who *is* infected then you can also
> catch *any*thing, whether it's a virus per se or not – Alzheimer's, muscu-
> lar dystrophy, hemophilia, leukemia, anorexia, diabetes, cancer,
> multiple sclerosis, cystic fibrosis, cerebral palsy, dyslexia, for Christ
> sakes – you can get dyslexia from *pussy.*
>
> (Ellis 1991: 5)

Yuppie politics

Bateman claims to be anti-apartheid, pro-family and anti-drug and, like other yuppies, believes that as a heterosexual white male he cannot contract AIDS. Yuppie Van Patten says: 'our chances of catching that are like zero zero zero zero point half a decimal percentage or something, and this no matter what kind of scumbag, slutbucket, horndog chick we end up boffing' (Ellis 1991: 34). When Bateman notices that yuppie Stash is looking miserable he surmises that Stash has simply been unable to get a reservation at Camol's Restaurant and comments: 'his net worth a pittance' (Ellis 1991: 13). In fact, we learn, Stash has just been diagnosed as suffering from AIDS. Bateman cannot be trusted on any level. At the start of the book somebody foolishly throws out a general question as to what the most pressing issues of the day might be. Bateman responds:

> 'Well, we have to end apartheid for one. And slow down the nuclear arms race, stop terrorism and world hunger. Ensure a strong national defense, prevent the spread of communism in Central America, work for a Middle East peace settlement, prevent US military involvement overseas. Now that's not to belittle our domestic problems, which are equally important, if not *more*. Better and more affordable long-term care for the elderly, control and find a cure for the AIDS epidemic, clean up environmental damage from toxic waste and pollution, improve the quality of primary and secondary education, strengthen laws to crack down on crime and illegal drugs. We also have to ensure that college education is affordable for the middle class and protect Social Security for senior citizens plus conserve natural resources and wilderness areas and reduce the influence of political action committees. [. . .] But economically we're still in a mess. We have to find a way to hold down the inflation rate and reduce the deficit. We also need to provide training and jobs for the unemployed as well as protect existing American jobs from unfair foreign imports. We have to make America the leader in new technology. At the same time we need to promote economic growth and business expansion and hold the line against federal income taxes and hold down interest rates while promoting opportunities for small businesses and controlling mergers and big corporate takeovers. [. . .] But we can't ignore our social need either. We have to stop people from abusing the welfare system. We have to provide food and shelter for the homeless and oppose racial discrimination and promote civil rights while also promoting equal rights for women but change the abortion laws to protect the right to life yet still somehow maintain women's freedom of choice. We have to encourage the influx of illegal immigrants. We

have to encourage a return to traditional values and curb graphic sex and violence on TV, in movies, in popular music, everywhere. Most importantly we have to promote general social concern and less materialism in young people.'

(Ellis 1991: 15)

This speech, as a parody of Ronald Reagan, is very good indeed. It starts out in mouthing liberal platitudes that few can object to, and then proceeds fairly smartly to an opposite and self-contradictory right-wing position. Coming from a Wall Street yuppie who specializes in acquisitions and mergers (the creation of unemployment), a regular drug user, a man who subscribes to *Playboy* and who frequently hires call-girls and prostitutes, who murders at least one homeless man and whose regular video loans (for masturbatory purposes) include titles such as *Ginger's Cunt*, *She-Male Reformatory*, *Pamela's Tight Fuckhole* and *Inside Lydia's Ass*, this is richly hypocritical.

Identifying yuppies

These Wall Street yuppies, for all their discussions about suits, shoes, ties, vests, wallets and cummerbunds, and the correct way to match accessories, all look alike – even to each other. Bateman is continually being mistaken for someone else and he often mistakes other people:

I trip out onto the street, bumping into Charles Murphy from Kidder Peabody or it could be Bruce Barker from Morgan Stanley, *whoever*, and he says 'Hey Kinsley'.

(Ellis 1991: 151)

At one point Bateman is mistaken for Marcus Halberstam and has to fake answers about his relationship with Marcia and his work on the Hawkins account. This device is used several times to good comic effect, but it also has a serious additional bonus for the novel. One hundred and sixty-one days after he says he murdered two prostitutes and Wall Street trader Paul Owen, Bateman notes:

There has been no word of bodies discovered in any of the city's four newspapers or on the local news; no hints of even a rumor floating around. I've gone so far as to ask people – dates, business acquaintances – over dinners, in the halls of Pierce & Pierce, if anyone has heard about two mutilated prostitutes found in Paul Owen's apartment. But like in some movie, no one has heard anything, has any idea what I'm talking about. There are other things to worry over.

(Ellis 1991: 367)

He also confesses to Evelyn, his fiancée, explaining the reasons why they cannot be married: 'My . . . my *need* to engage in . . . homicidal behavior on a massive scale cannot be, um, corrected.' However, either this is not what Bateman says, or she does not hear him. She replies: 'If you are going to start in again on why I should have breast implants, I'm leaving' (Ellis 1991: 338). He had previously tried to tell Daisy that he was interested in 'murders and executions', but again she was hardly listening to him and thought he said 'mergers and acquisitions' (Ellis 1991: 206).

At one point Bateman telephones a colleague and confesses. However, when he meets Harold Carnes, the man for whom this confession was intended, Carnes mistakes Bateman for someone called Davis and assumes the message was a joke. When Bateman presses Carnes, he says:

'Davis [. . .] I am not one to bad-mouth anyone, your joke *was* amusing. But come on man, you had one fatal flaw: Bateman's such a bloody ass-kisser, such a brown-nosing goody-goody, that I couldn't fully appreciate it. Otherwise it was amusing [. . .] Why else would Evelyn Richards dump him? You know, really. He could barely *pick up* an escort girl, let alone . . . What was it you said he did to her?'

(Ellis 1991: 387)

Bateman's confession not only goes badly awry, but Carnes then tells him that it is impossible that anybody has killed Paul Owen because he had dinner with Owen 'twice' just a few days ago in London. Bateman is also visited in his office by a detective investigating Owen's disappearance, but the detective says he suspects Owen is just avoiding his girlfriend since he owes her money and has been seen in London by a yuppie called Stephen Hughes. However the detective also reveals that upon investigation Hughes had mistaken Hubert Ainsworth for Owen (Ellis 1991: 273).

The effect of this confusion, combined with Bateman's admission that the deaths have not been reported in the press, throws the whole narrative into doubt. Has Bateman really been committing murders, or has he been imagining them? Is he a reliable narrator? We only ever have his word. Did Carnes have lunch with Owen in London, or did Carnes mistake Owen for someone else? The possibility that Bateman has been imagining his murderous adventures is available to us because there are several details and jumps in the text that allow us to feel he may have been leading a double life, or just fantasizing (Ellis 1991: 288, 303, 327). These are textual ambiguities which Mary Harron's film *American Psycho* (2000) was able to use very effectively.

Responses to the book

There are questions that each individual reader will have to consider: Is the book pornographic? Is it shocking? Asked if he considered the book to be shocking or offensive Ellis said:

> You have to ask yourself: what is offensive? Everyone has their own different list of what is offensive and what is not. I don't think there is anything offensive that you can do in writing. There's nothing you can do that is going to offend me in a book unless it's really stupid writing and it's a really stupid idea for a book or you've got moronic dialogue or stuff that really rings false. That will offend me. But in terms of subject – you can write about pedophiles, someone who slays thousands of people, a corrupt politician – none of that is going to offend me. But if you really handle it poorly on an aesthetic level, then I'm going to be probably more upset. But I don't think there's any topic you can touch on that is going to be offensive to me [. . .] I think it is very hard because of how we've been pulverized by visual images to be genuinely shocked by what we read in a book. I find it very rare to come across something where I'm gasping. I might gasp at some revelation that happens in the book, but it's rarely a scene of sexuality or a scene of violence that makes me freak out. It's usually something more subtle than that.
>
> (Clarke 1996/98)

Asked how and in what ways *American Psycho* had affected his career, Ellis did not talk of responsibility or of the death threats and protests:

> In some ways it damaged my reputation. Then on the same level in other ways, it completely enhanced it. In the end, it completely changed whatever reputation I had and pushed it in a different direction. It also made me very distrustful of the publishing industry. I'm much more wary of editors now [. . .] I'm much more wary of how the business side of publishing works.
>
> (Clarke 1996/98)

It is legitimate to ask what literary merits this book has. To a great extent the answer lies with the way the satire is connected to the murder and torture.

Ellis said it seemed logical to him that one of the yuppies would be driven mad by the obsession with status and that this would 'incite him into becoming a murderer' (Clarke 1996/98). But is this wisdom after the event? And is this how the novel actually works? Are the details of the killings and Bateman's imagination intimately linked to Wall Street? Does the book take the yuppie lifestyle to its logical conclusion?

It is satirically apt, for example, to say that there is a fine line between sharp business practice and outright theft, and it is legitimate to make a 'killing' on Wall Street. However, while we know almost nothing of Bateman's life before the novel begins it is clear that his father was very wealthy, that Bateman was well educated, that Bateman need not work for a living and that he was probably dangerously disturbed before he started to work on Wall Street. His money will buy anything. So why does he need to kill? What is the logic of his killing? It may be that power interests him more than anything else, but why is this yuppie, unlike all the others, a serial killer? He may have been drawn to Wall Street by the opportunities to exercise his power but Wall Street does not seem to be the root of his problem. It may be incidental that this psychopath works on Wall Street, but on the other hand it may be no accident that this psychopath is a yuppie.

While the satirical comedy is superbly observed, the dialogue malicious, the sex detailed, and the murder scenes suitably gruesome, the main problem with the book is that the themes of murder and money, although they meet in Bateman, are not integrated sufficiently to cast light on one another. There is a connection, but we do not know enough about what the yuppies do on Wall Street to be able to connect these things closely. While the satire and the murders make a nice political point, it could also be said they hit a target that, as a socio-political phenomenon, had already disappeared. On the other hand, as Ellis says:

> Patrick Bateman can exist at anytime. Patrick Bateman is an example of what Hannah Arendt called 'the banality of evil'. That's basically what he is. He could have existed a hundred years ago (he probably existed five hundred years ago). He'll probably exist five hundred years from now. He's just an example of the constantness of evil. He might be a creature of the eighties with all the trappings that implies, but I think he's really a creature of eternity. Man doesn't necessarily change for the better depending on the decade, or depending upon how ten years have passed. I think man is born and is corrupted and is always capable of badness. Capable of goodness too, but badness gets more attention.
>
> (Clarke 1996/98)

11 Between Poland and Germany

Günter Grass, *The Tin Drum*

World War II was not one war, but a great many small wars. After the war many Germans wanted nothing more than to forget the whole episode and return to normality as quickly as possible and by the late 1950s Germany had been 'normalized'.

Günter Grass, however, saw the war from a different perspective. He felt that in the postwar years there were far too many unrepentant Nazis in positions of power, and far too much power concentrated again in the hands of either the prewar bankers and businessmen who had co-operated with Hitler, or in the hands of people who were clearly right-wing sympathizers.

From the late 1960s Grass was an outspoken champion for the Social Democrats: he campaigned for better contacts between east and west and better understanding in German–Polish relations. In short Grass, while he could not bring back the dead, could at least remember what had been lost in the war and could try to undo in his writing some of the damage the Nazis had done.

This chapter looks at Grass's sense of national and political responsibility. It shows his attempts to reveal that Nazism fed on other invisible wars of discontent, and to demonstrate that these persisted after 1945.

It revisits issues of identity, tradition, history, authenticity and language from previous chapters.

Danzig is a city of fable. It is fabled in that it no longer figures on the maps of Europe. It is fabled in that it is celebrated in the fabulous novels of Günter Grass. It is fabled in that in both real life and Grass's novels it was a place where people were 'different', where things happened. Grass's massive talent often obscures the use to which he puts the city; his fabulous characters often distract the reader from the fact that, buried within the fable, Grass has created a cumulative picture of middle-class life in the city up to the end of World War II. It is a picture which is brutal and painstakingly honest in its dissection of the secret inner life of these people. It is a portrait that chronicles the selfishness, the wilful folly, of a people who brought destruction down upon themselves. Yet it is also a record of the richness and variety of the city's human potential and the gravity of its destruction in 1945.

Danzig, the world of Grass's childhood, has been lost to him in several senses. Through the passage of time he has grown to adulthood, but also, through exile from the place of his birth, by its physical destruction in the final days of the war, and by the loss of the city's territory to Poland, Grass is separated from the subject of his writings. Since the lifetime of Danzig lay before the defeat of Hitler, and before Grass's 're-education' in the American POW camps, and since the ending of his childhood was almost simultaneous with the death of Danzig and the Third Reich, the city is also an ambiguous symbol of loss, of weakness, of the failure of the Weimar democracy, of the folly of the Nazi solution that lurked within that Weimar failure and within German history as a whole. For Grass, Danzig is lost, lamented, longed for and feared.

Conjuring up the past

Oskar and his drum, the main characters of the novel *The Tin Drum* (1961), are fitting symbols. Drums were a favourite Nazi symbol of martial masculinity, and Hitler often described himself as a drummer, drumming up support for the great leader who would come after him. In the same way that Oskar drums up memories in his hospital bed to create the text of the novel, so Grass re-creates Danzig on his typewriter. The images that both Oskar and Grass conjure are often ugly and frequently they are emotionally manipulative:

> Perhaps if I rubbed my typewriter superficially with onion juice, it might communicate an intimation of the onion smell which in those years contaminated all Germany, West Prussia and Langfuhr, Osterzeile as well as Westerzeile, preventing the smell of corpses from taking over completely.
>
> (Grass 1963: 130)

Grass undercuts any cosy nostalgia about the city. He never divorces it from its unsavoury context of the German eastern Marches, the national conflict so central to Prussian Ostpolitik, nor the German and Polish national identities that developed in those lands.

The epic technique allows Grass to puncture some of the mysteries of the Nazi era – and through them the inheritance of the Prussian East. It also allows him to illuminate some of the conflicts peculiar to the German–Polish borderlands, particularly the struggle for national identity. Herbert Truczynski's back charts his experiences on the Sweden Bar in Neufahrwasser. His scars bear ample testimony to the various conflicts of the interwar years and the legacy of the Versailles Treaty. Oskar learns that every scar has a story. Oskar presses a scar and Herbert talks:

> Oh that one! That was a Ukrainian. He was having a row with a character from Gdingen. First they were sitting at the same table like brothers. And then the character from Gdingen says: Russki. The Ukrainian wasn't going to take that lying down; if there was one thing he didn't want to be, it was Russki. [. . .] I had to separate the two of them, soft and gentle the way I always do. Well Herbert has his hands full. At this point the Ukrainian calls me a Water Polack, and the Polack, who spends his time hauling up muck on a dredger, calls me something that sounds like Nazi. Well, my boy, you know Herbert Truczynski: a minute later the guy from the dredger, pasty faced guy, looks like a stoker, is lying doubled up by the coatroom. I'm just beginning to tell the Ukrainian what the difference is between a Water Polack and a citizen of Danzig when he gives it to me from behind – and that's the scar.
>
> (Grass 1961: 179)

The whole legacy of nineteenth-century nationalism and national struggle underlies this passage, but Grass works to expose the simplifications of the nation-state, to question the labels 'German' and 'Polish'. Herbert is a Pole in a German-speaking Free City, but he is clearly a loyal citizen of Danzig rather than a disaffected nationalist. From the insecure vantage point of his own ethnic background Grass asks awkward questions about the more local loyalties that go to make up the larger loyalty of the nation-state. He asks what it is to be Kaszubian, or even part Kaszubian, when at various times in their history both Germany and Poland have expanded their territory and definition of themselves to include peoples who did not regard themselves as either Polish or German. For the most part Grass speaks only of the Kaszubians, but there are other peoples involved in a similar fashion: Kosznavians, Mazurians, Silesians, Pomeranians, Wends and Sorbs. Grass reminds us that each large nation is made up of a series of smaller nations – some of which have a historical memory of their own – who disappear inconveniently slowly, who for the most part are invisible to 'official' history, and yet whose history (such as it might be) is still not identical with the larger, visible and legitimate entity of the nation-state that contains them.

Grass and identity

But who are these Kaszubians, from whom both Grass and Oskar claim descent? The Kaszubians are one of Europe's almost invisible, not quite history-less peoples. They speak a dialect of the long-vanished Polabian language, which had been closely related to the Sorbian, Wendish, Serbian and Polish languages. The Kaszubes were part of the ancient complex of Slav tribes that occupied Pomerania and the southern shores of the Baltic right up to the Danish border some time around the sixth century AD. Eventually the area occupied by the Kaszubians shrank to a narrow strip of land running north to south, parallel to the coastline around Danzig. By accident or design the area they occupied was almost exactly that designated as 'The Polish Corridor' after the Treaty of Versailles: nowadays Kaszubia is vaguely defined as a damp sandy strip of farmland lying west of Gdansk, and centred on the Polish town of Kartuzy.

In spite of everything that history subsequently threw at them in the form of Scandinavian, Swedish, German, Polish, Prussian and Russian invasions, the Kaszubians have remained in the place they first chose to settle. All the other Slav dialects of Pomerania – indeed with the exception of the Sorbs and Wends of East Germany, all the other Slav peoples who once co-occupied the great north German plain right up to the mouth of the Elbe – have withered away and been absorbed into German nationality, leaving hardly a trace. The Kaszubians were, and remain, insular, agrarian people thoroughly resistant to change. Sir Robert Donald, writing in the late 1920s characterized them thus:

> The Cashubes remain a somewhat primitive community. They have no ideals. They are devoid of initiative in political action, are content to be led, and are easily exploited. They want to cultivate their fields; to live peacefully under conditions which suit their habits and characteristics.
>
> (Donald n.d.: 32)

By the end of the nineteenth century the Kaszubians had long since been deprived of the more fertile agricultural land. Where they were not serfs on the larger estates they were peasant smallholders, farm labourers, market-women and fishermen. Those who worked the land grew rye and potatoes (the area is too damp for wheat), beetroot, apples; they fattened a few pigs and large flocks of geese. The end of serfdom came late to Pomerania, mainly because of the conservative Junker landowners who dominated the area. For the Kaszubes released from service on the land in the 1890s, for those freed from the land anchor of smallholdings, and for those who wished to migrate or simply to trade their produce, the natural focus of Kaszubian population drift was neither Warsaw nor Berlin, but Danzig.

Understandably, throughout the years of Polish partition the Kaszubians had been uninterested in the fate of Poland and initially had been satisfied by lenient Prussian rule. Later, as the Prussians revised their statutes governing the activity of Jews and revoked laws preventing usury, the Kaszubian farmers began to find themselves heavily in debt. As Frederick's policies in the eastern lands turned into those of Bismarck, the Catholic Kaszubians found further cause for alarm. The Prussians, in an effort to Germanize their eastern territories, restricted the use of the Polish language and made no distinction between Polish and Kaszubian. The Kaszubians came under strong pressure to Germanize, but it took them a long time to see an ally in the Poles.

For their part the Poles regarded the Kaszubians as something of an agrarian joke, since while the Poles had an enormous, highly literary culture behind them, the Kaszubians had almost no literature at all; worse, the Kaszubians had almost no sense of common identity, no political representation or ambition. Whereas the Poles of East Prussia refused to sell their land to Germans, the Kaszubians in distress would sell to the highest bidder, regardless of language or nationality. The Poles took advantage of Kaszubian naïveté by buying up over 35,000 acres of Kaszubian land between 1896 and 1905 as part of their struggle to counter the effects of Germanization. Increasingly hysterical efforts to Germanize the borderlands slowly forced the Kaszubians to see their survival as lying with the Poles rather than with the Germans; that is, the continued existence of the Kaszubians as Kaszubians was possible only within a resurrected Polish state and certainly not within the increasingly tight strait-jacket of German identity.

The Kaszubians suffered Germanization alongside the Poles until the Polish state was reconstructed in 1918. But being part of the inter-war Polish state did the Kaszubians little good. They found that tariff barriers prevented their produce from reaching traditional German markets, and that everything they could grow, the Poles could grow much more cheaply. Predictably the Poles paid Kaszubian culture and language scant and grudging attention. In 1939 the Germans invaded Poland, abolished the Polish Corridor and reincorporated Danzig into the Reich. Nazi policy in the eastern borderlands descended in a straight line from the policies of Bismarck and Frederick of Prussia: just as their predecessors had done, the Nazis set about Germanizing the east. But whereas the Prussians had been content to absorb or expel Slavs and Jews, the Nazis set out to purge what they could not immediately control. Backing the Nazi efforts at Germanization was the technology of the gas chamber and the incinerator.

A worm's eye view of identity

Grass's Kaszubian origins give him a uniquely ironical, worm's eye view of what his more confident and powerful neighbours are up to. This irony is a constant thread of sanity: the blue-eyed, blond-haired Oskar is a German-speaking German. But then, perhaps not. He is also a German-speaking, blue-eyed, blond-haired part Kaszubian. And given that his presumptive father is a Pole rather than a German, he might also be a German-speaking, blue-eyed, blond-haired Kaszubian Pole. In fact Oskar could be German or Polish or Kaszubian or any combination of these three. Oskar's grandmother is Kaszubian, but as Oskar tells us, the Kaszubians 'Got themselves Germanized':

> The old folks had been turned into Germans. They were Poles no longer and spoke Kashubian only in their dreams. German Nationals, Group 3, they were called. Moreover, Hedwig Bronski, Jan's widow, had married a Baltic German who was a local peasant leader in Ramkau. Petitions were already under way, which when approved, would entitle Marga and Stephen Bronski to take the name of their stepfather Ehlers.
>
> (Grass 1961: 301)

Under the Nazis there was a *Volksliste* which categorized everybody in terms of racial origin and standing within the Reich. There were four main categories. First were the *Reichsdeutsch* – Germans born within the Reich; second were the *Volksdeutsch* – Germans born outside the Reich or those who could claim German ancestors for the preceding three generations; third were the *Nichtdeutsch* – non-Jewish non-Germans who might be suitable for Germanization. In this last category the Nazis usually thought of the Kaszubians and Poles from Pomerania, Mazuria and Silesia as possible future Germans, if not in this generation then in the next, and accordingly they allowed Kaszubians to become Germanized on paper, or they simply stole 'racially promising material' – children – from schools, nurseries and homes for education in special Germanization camps. In practical terms the idea that a Kaszubian adult could become Germanized was yet another Nazi legalism. In reality it made no real difference at all since they merely shifted about a little in the subsection to which they had been assigned. Neither they nor their children, nor their grandchildren, would have become 'proper' Germans under Nazi law. The fourth category on the list was *Juden*: Jews.

Grass mocks the whole mentality – and the Nazi version is, like the apartheid system of South Africa, only one of the extreme forms – whereby the identity, the worth, the social standing, the security of individuals and whole ethnic groups can be altered and reversed by the stroke of a pen. Oskar's maternal grandmother takes the whole thing a step further and defends her gift of a goose with the words: 'Don't make such a fuss, Alfred. She's no Kashubian goose, she's a German National bird and tastes just like before the war' (Grass 1961: 302). National identity, it seems, extends even to the poultry. They all share in a change of status. It even affects the flavour of the goose.

Identity and language

It is a linguistic mix too. In *From the Diary of a Snail* (1974) Stomma and his family spoke Kaszubian at home, German at school and Polish to visitors. After 1918 their village was ceded to Poland, so Lisbeth Stomma spoke Kaszubian at home, Polish at school and German to visitors. Uncertainty extends to family names too, and the variety and history of the surnames in Grass's novels are another indication that the nation-state is a far more varied creature than its surface uniformity would at first allow. 'Putty', one of the leading members of Oskar's gang of 'Dusters', is in fact the son of Von Puttkamer, of mixed Polish, Pomeranian and Prussian descent. Tulla Pokriefke, who appears both in *The Tin Drum* (1961) and in *Dog Years* (1965), is ostensibly German, but her family are in fact Kosznavian – another of the almost invisible tribal survivals from the Slav–German borderlands – and in Polish her surname means 'saucepan-lid'. In Grass's novels people change their names with the ebb and flow of power: just what a family name might be at any point depends on who is in power at the time and precisely where the national borders are placed. In *Cat and Mouse* Grass wrote:

> The fashion for Germanizing Polish sounding names ending in *ki* or *ke* or *a* – like Formella – was taken up by lots of people in those days: Lewandowski became Lengnisch; Mr Olczewski, our butcher had himself metamorphosed into Mr Ohlwein; Jurgen Kupka's parents wanted to take the East Prussian name of Kupkat, but their petition, heaven knows why, was rejected.
>
> (Grass 1963: 124)

By daring to show the process by which Slavonic names become Germanized, Grass is mocking the basis of Nazi ideology and practice in the eastern borderlands. He is also questioning the possibility of an ethnically pure German Reich, a pure German race, and ultimately questioning the German identity itself. It is no accident that the Nazi Sawatzki in *Dog Years* should have a Germanized version of a Polish name (in Polish Sawacki), since that in itself is a way of exploring the insecurities that the Nazis managed to turn into a national phobia, and also a way of insisting on the rich ethnic mix that made up the borderlands before 1945.

In *From the Diary of a Snail* uncertainty, plurality, variety extends especially to geography and to place names:

> I really ought to go into the statistics of history at this point and say something about the changing linguistic mixture in the villages of the Karthaus district. When was Klobschin called Klobocin, and why was Klobocin called Klobschin? When and how often was the hamlet of Neuendorf, west of Turmberg, called Nowawies in Polish? Why does Seereson, which lies between Karthaus and Zuckau, appear as Derisno when first mentioned in 1241, as Sehereson beginning in 1570, and alternately as Seroson and Serosen in the period after 1789. Why in the nineteenth century did it become Seeresen, though concomitantly it appears time and time again in Polish and Kashubian as Dzierzazno? Such is history as its fallout affects the countryside.
>
> (Grass 1974: 137)

Germans and Jews

Grass has good reason to mock. The strait-jacket of identity imposed after Yalta and Potsdam was but a variation of the uniformity that the Nazis had sought to impose and one which undermined the best but misguided intentions of the Versailles politicians. Ironies abound. Arguably the sense of Polish nationality, intense Polish nationalism and national identity cutting across regional, class and dialect differences were all the result of German efforts to eradicate these very things. But Poland only became a monocultural, monolingual society as a result of the defeat of Hitler; both Polish and German national identities were simplified by Hitler's defeat. It is a lunatic world, yet it is a world which Grass delights in disassembling for us. It is not something he does without bitterness or rancour, but rather with resigned patience:

> That's how it is with the Kashubes. They always get hit on the head [. . .] the Kashubes are no good at moving. Their business is to stay where they are and hold out their heads for everybody else to hit, because we're not real Poles and we're not real Germans, and if you're a Kashube, you're not good enough for the Germans or the Polacks. They want everything full measure.
>
> (Grass 1961: 416)

National identity is some endless conundrum, some labyrinthine joke. And nowhere is this more apparent than in Grass's treatment of the relationship between Germans and Jews in *Dog Years*. There the seemingly irreconcilable opposites are posed: the Master Race meets the Chosen People. Except that the Germans are not real Germans and the Jews are not real Jews. The cry 'Sheeny, Sheeny, Sheeny' is echoed and answered by the cry 'Nazi, Nazi, Nazi'. It is an ugly equation. There is a weird symmetry at work in the relationship between Matern, the sometime maybe Nazi, and Amsel, the sometime maybe Jew. Matern and Amsel are literally blood brothers. They are linked in ways they do not understand, in much the same way that the history of Israel is linked to the history of nationalism in Germany and Poland.

The growth of Zionist opinion as it manifested itself in Germany, Poland and Russia at the end of the nineteenth century was arguably the product of traditional intolerance exacerbated by the increasing pressure of industrialization and the homogenization of the labour and product markets of the various national blocks working through uncertainty about national identity and loyalties. The processes of industrialization increased pressure on all the 'marginal' identities either to conform to national norms – as the Kaszubians seem to have done – or to resist that conformity in the way that Zionism did.

Grass is interested in a relationship that works through the insecurities of both parties, in their zigzag opposition, competition and outright adoration of each other. Grass is interested in the idea of the Jew, the idea of the Nazi. Neither of Grass's two main Jewish characters – Amsel in *Dog Years* and Herman Ott in *From the Diary of a Snail* – is really Jewish at all. Ott simply is not a Jew: Amsel's ethnic Jewish origins are so distant that they have no meaning for him. Yet they are seen to be Jews by those around them. Their Jewishness consists of their opposition to the dominant political and social trends of their society; it has more to do with available social roles than with ethnicity – the enemy within, scapegoat, outcast, foreigner, competitor, traitor, conscience.

Like other forms of national identity in the borderlands, 'Jewishness' is a threat when it is not a convenience; it is a threat that, unlike a Polish or a German identity, has no army or navy to back it up. The Jews had almost by tradition been inserted into the slow-growing economies of eastern Europe to the advantage and disgust of those higher up the social hierarchy, and to the disadvantage and frustration of those lower down the social scale. As such Jews were vulnerable to attack from all sides. It is an interesting paradox that while the Nazis were supposed to be supermen, their appeal was to Germans who felt themselves to be far from super; Nazi support came from ordinary Germans who looked to the Nazis and to their refined spearhead, the SS, as their models. While Nazi propaganda stressed the superman image, Germany was said to be under threat from the *Untermenschen*, from the lesser and inferior races. How could that be? Clearly the relationship between these ideas is exceedingly complex.

Grass the committed writer

Grass is profoundly committed to his own time and his own place. He implicates the reader in the story he has to tell. The characters he creates are all hopelessly entwined in the events of a history that their ambition and uncertainty have helped to create. Their habits of thought have delivered them into a chaos of their own making, into an uncertainty of a different order from anything they have ever known. There is a powerful pedagogical streak in Grass too, and the fact that by the time he had begun work as a novelist his own children were beginning to ask him questions about his past and his activities under the Nazis helped to give his work a very clear style, direction and purpose.

By insisting on the continuities between the Third Reich and the postwar West German state, Grass produced a series of merciless portraits of a society brought face to face with its own inner doubts and uncertainties, with the results of its attempts to force a bloody resolution on its neighbours, and with its overpowering wish both to forget and to rewrite its history. He stressed that although the whole of Germany shared in the moral surrender of Hitler's legitimate rise to power, not all those who supported the NSDAP could be called Nazis. In Danzig the Nazi supporters were ordinary people who walked their dogs, conducted illicit affairs, ran scout troops, went fishing, cut holes in the ice to bathe in the sea, ran grocery shops, played the trumpet – the same people who, if they survived the war, would take advantage of the 1948 Currency Reform and later West German rearmament to spoon cake to their dogs at Kempinski's restaurant in West Berlin and claim that they had always been against that chap Hitler:

> I did not speak about the black demons who destroyed the Germans and were like devils and so on – all this mystification. I spoke against this. I said: 'All this happened in daylight'. And I showed my class, where I come from, with all their unfulfilled wishes. And no party, neither the Communists nor the Social Democrats took care over these people, so it was very easy for Hitler to take over these middle class people – lower middle class people mostly. This was the background I knew very well. And I also knew very well their dreams, their operatic dreams. Hitler was a figure they waited for.
>
> (Grass 1984)

In many ways Grass's novels conform to the basic pattern of 'Exile Literature'. The sense of loss is overwhelming, the memory is sharp, the ability to recall is total. What is missing is self-pity. In postwar Germany self-pity and exile were very closely linked to the cloying emotions of very German notions of home, fatherland and comfort, *gemütlichkeit*, a sense of order and fitness of things, a sense of rightness – and through that to a sense of identity, of place and function within an ordered and secure community. Given the dangers of these emotions Grass's balancing act becomes all the more difficult. It is no accident that the secondary growth of kitsch art in Germany coincided with the growth of the Nazi Party. The easy sentiment and the surrender of both taste and responsibility in art go hand in hand with the same things in the political sphere. Kitsch is an art and politics of easy mass appeal. That is, it revels in the collapse of standards. Kitsch is an art form for the surrender of taste and sensitive discrimination; it is an art of easy forms, easy sentiments, swim-with-the-tide conformity. Grass has to combat this powerful undercurrent lest his own works become appropriated by some simplistic revisionism or by exile-sentiment – a very real fear in West Germany both before and after reunification.

History and repetition

Grass's narrators are always the wounded, the weary and the wary speaking out for those still to come:

> What had taken seven hundred years to build burned down in three days. Yet this was not the first fire to descend on the city of Danzig. For centuries Pomerellians, Brandenburgers, Teutonic Knights, Poles, Swedes, and a second time Swedes, Frenchmen, Prussians, and Russians, even Saxons, had made history by deciding every few years that Danzig was worth burning. And now it was the Russians, Poles, Germans, and Englishmen, all at once who were burning the city's Gothic bricks for the hundredth time.
>
> (Grass 1961: 389)

Grass laments the loss of the city, but he also laments the stupidity that led to that loss. His line is that if there is one thing we learn from history it is simply that we do not learn from history. While he castigates the decadence and moral bankruptcy of the Danzigers who supported Hitler, and the West Germans who have still not renounced the aims of the Nazis, never once has Grass allowed himself to lapse into emotive pleas that Danzig and all the other German lands lost to Poland in 1945 should be returned: never once has Grass given in to the calls of the German Exiles' Unions, or acquiesced in Chancellor Kohl's barely veiled promise that one day the Polish city of Gdansk would be reclaimed for Germany as the ancient city of Danzig.

A Kaszubian – and even more a German-speaking part Kaszubian – is on the margin of both German and Polish society. It is a worm's eye view that does not attract critical attention simply because it is an angle on national life that does not accord with 'mainstream' cultural and linguistic experience. Where Grass's unique viewpoint is noticed at all, it is only to be dismissed as exotic but basically marginal to the interests both of German and of Polish readers – and of course through them marginal to the official interests of both states. And yet it is clear from the popularity of *The Tin Drum* alone that Grass works on his readers – not only Polish and German, but all readers – in ways that they don't quite understand, can't quite drag to light.

The view from the margin

Grass demonstrates that it is often those elements on the margins of a cultural and linguistic identity, those elements not fully integrated into the mainstream of social and political collective ambition, those who are not fully under the control of generally agreed social mores – the socially, politically deprived, the ethnic minorities, women, the sexual rebels, religious minorities, political outcasts, even some professional intellectuals – all the creatures of the margin, who show any real sense of observing what a society is and what it does.

The artists of the margin – people like Milan Kundera, John Berger, Václav Havel, Josef Skvorecky, Gyorgy Konrád, Ryszard Kapuściński, Gabriel Garcia Marquez, Wole Soyinka, Chinua Achebe – often have a real sense of how power derives within a society, how the inner logic of a society operates. These people of the margin are not so overwhelmed by a society that they submerge their identity and lapse into material accumulation, selective amnesia or perplexed silence. However, just as a society makes these people – at one end of the spectrum the inarticulate drunks and drug addicts, at the other poets, visionaries and philosophers – into potential revolutionaries, so it also isolates them and renders them powerless by turning their marginality into a weapon against them; they are rendered parodies of themselves, they are treated as freaks, their work is explained away as entertainment, or as divine but irrelevant fantasy.

Grass is part of a fraternity of writers who face the great powers, victorious histories and larger languages from eccentric and often repressed cultures, and who because of this have an obligation to confirm their continued existence and an obligation to say how they see the world. The fact that 'official' history, east and west, north and south, capitalist and communist, does not want them to say how they see the world makes their task all the more urgent.

12 African reality

Wole Soyinka, 'The writer in a modern African state'

Sometimes a politico-literary movement develops which seems to answer the most urgent questions of the day. It takes a rare talent and a brave writer to think differently. Political correctness was one such movement. Negritude was another. Negritude is still a potent item on the political agenda since it underpins movements like the Black Panthers and the Nation of Islam, and is still important to many politicians in Africa.

Nigerian writer and Nobel Prize winner Wole Soyinka was never thrilled by the promise of Negritude. His willingness to challenge Negritude as part of his definition of what an African writer's responsibilities might be, are the basis of the next chapter.

This chapter also revisits issues of identity and the duties of citizenship, and opens up some awkward areas of political correctness.

It is difficult to grasp much of Soyinka's work outside the context of his arguments with Africans about Africa and what African writing might be. Much of his early writing was part of a debate about Negritude. Although the Negritude movement is not what it once was, its ideas, fragmented and mutated, are still with us, and this is a debate to which Soyinka often returns in his later work.

Negritude

The word 'Negritude' was coined by the poet Aimé Césaire in 1939 to mean 'the collective Negro-African personality'. Leopold Sedar Senghor gave the movement further political legitimacy and literary impetus in the 1940s and 1950s with his poetry on the themes of the experience of a great cultural awakening for black people everywhere, the 'bitter taste of liberty', the problems of using a colonial language, the protective guiding influence of ancestors, the devastation of the African culture by Europe, the increasing distance from old ways of thinking and feeling, the warmth, beauty and generosity of African women.

Senghor was on a quest to restore harmony and unity, to overcome alienation of the spirit. His poems showed the problems of a Francophone, western-educated African elite coming to terms with the idea of independence, adapting its cultural heritage to western military and economic power whilst at the same time attempting to preserve as much as possible from the past. Senghor did not condemn everything European and was clearly attracted to the material culture, and for many readers searching for signposts Senghor's poetry was confusing. However, it was the poet Leon Damas who summed up the main thrust of the movement by writing poetry and essays that indicated he hated living on the margins of European culture and wealth, especially since Europe continued to ransack Africa for whatever it could find.

Negritude insisted that before Europeans arrived Africa had enjoyed a history largely without conflict. The implication was that if Africa could keep Europe at a distance it had a future without conflict too, since to be black was to inherit a perfected identity. Negritude appealed particularly to black intellectuals educated in France, people who felt themselves assimilated but only to a certain degree, and who felt the need to give the system of values they acquired in Europe an African content. They stressed the need for an antithesis to white values, a reaction against materialism and individualism into an assumed African moral idealism and superiority of community.

The Negritude movement was populated mainly by members of the educated urban elite, people with little or no real contact with village life. This new African intellectual leadership was geographically diverse, belonged to no common cultural tradition and faced the task of weaving a commonality out of a very complex variety of local traditions and little-documented cultures, and out of a European colonial legacy ill-fitted to these tasks. Negritude was a very literary affair and distinguished itself by concentrating on 'black emotions' and ideas. Though it was puzzling to Anglophone Africa (the word is not recorded in English until the 1950s), in Francophone Africa Negritude was linked with the discovery that Africans were not only black, but also not white. It was to become massively important in connecting the ideas of a developing pan-African, anti-colonial, anti-European, non-European intellectual fraternity as the poets of Negritude struggled to rediscover black African dignity.

Franz Fanon (1925–61) was one of the most influential political thinkers and writers behind Negritude. He stressed that the impact of Europe had been much more subtle than many supposed. He made it clear that getting rid of the colonialists was not an end in itself, but was only the start of a much longer process. Fanon appreciated just how much the Third World depended on the First World. He sensed the power and attractiveness of the European lifestyle, he understood the range of Europe's economic systems, the ambitions Europe fostered in its ex-colonial black elite, and the military power of the USA and Europe. Fanon warned of the dangers of decolonization for an untutored national consciousness. He warned that African leaders who fostered simplistic 'black attitudes' and appealed to notions of tribal superiority or to a simplified Muslim or African identity would force Africa to pay a very high price for independence (Fanon 1965a; 1965b; 1967; 1970).

Wole Soyinka and Negritude

Wole Soyinka arrived on the literary scene at the crucial moment when the claims of the Negritude movement were first tested against the actuality of African independence. Soyinka was born in Abeakuta, in the Yoruba region of western Nigeria in 1934 or 1935. He was educated at Government College, Ibadan, then at University College, Ibadan, before going to England, to Leeds University, where he graduated in English. He worked as a play reader at the Royal Court, then in 1960 returned to Nigeria to become Research Fellow in Drama at Ibadan University.

Soyinka's play *Dance of the Forests* celebrated Nigerian Independence in October 1960. His first novel *The Interpreters* (1965) won the Jock Campbell Award for Commonwealth Literature, and in that same year he became a lecturer in English at Lagos University. Shortly afterwards he was accused of holding up a radio station and forcing it to broadcast a taped message to the Nigerian electorate, though charges were later dropped. In August 1967, at the start of the Nigerian civil war, Soyinka was arrested and he was kept in solitary confinement until October 1969. He was appointed Overseas Research Fellow at Churchill College, Cambridge, 1974–6, and then returned to Nigeria to teach Comparative Literature at the University of Ife. He was awarded the Nobel Prize for Literature in 1986 – the first African to receive the award.

It is perhaps not surprising that the Negritude movement tried to claim Soyinka. His poem 'Telephone conversation' (1963), based on his student experience in Leeds, clearly hit a white target:

> The price seemed reasonable, location
> Indifferent. The landlady swore she lived
> Off premises. Nothing remained
> But self confession. 'Madam,' I warned,

'I hate a wasted journey – I am African.'
Silence. Silenced transmission of
Pressurized good breeding. Voice, when it came,
Lipstick coated, long gold-rolled
Cigarette-holder pipped. Caught I was, foully.
'HOW DARK?' . . . I had not misheard . . . 'ARE YOU LIGHT
OR VERY DARK?'

(Moore and Beier 1973: 144)

However, Soyinka's other early poems, 'Death in the dawn', 'Civilian and
soldier', 'Prisoner', 'Season', made it clear his vision of Africa had little to
do with skin colour. He was concerned with African humanity, its failings,
patterns, ambitions and limitations.

When Negritude poets attempted to claim him as one of them he said
he saw no sense in what they were doing: 'Why do you have to proclaim
your Negritude – does the tiger proclaim its tigritude?' Soyinka noted that
Negritude had not made any serious effort to found or create a specifically
black system of values. Instead it merely stood white racism on its head
(Soyinka 1976: 63). He emphasized that as far as he was concerned Negritude had inadvertently painted itself into a corner. While it failed to
demolish the idea that analytical thought (invented by Europeans) was a
mark of high human development, it had concentrated on emphasizing,
not that Africans were just as capable of analytical thought, but that
Africans had something else to offer the world. What that something was,
apart from 'intuitive understanding, dance rhythm', could hardly be speci-
fied since it was still coming into being. This, he said, reduced the African
contribution to world history to an inarticulate racial splutter, and left the
myth of European supremacy unchallenged:

> Negritude accepted one of the most commonplace blasphemies of
> racism, that the black man has nothing between his ears, and pro-
> ceeded to subvert the power of poetry to glorify this fabricated
> justification of European cultural domination. Suddenly we were
> exhorted to give a cheer for those who never invented anything, a
> cheer for those who never explored the oceans. The truth, however, is
> that there isn't any such creature. An even more distressing deduction
> which escaped the euphoricists of such negativism is that they, the
> poets, had turned themselves into laudators of creative truncation.
> They suggest something which is indeed alien to the African world-
> view: that there are watertight categories of the creative spirit, that
> creativity is not one smooth flowing source of human regeneration.

(Soyinka 1976: 129)

The promise of independence

Nigeria's new leaders fully expected to solve all their country's problems as soon as the colonial rulers departed. Just after independence Azikwe, Governor General of Nigeria, at a London meeting of the African Organizations Committee, said everyone should realize that Africa, in spite of its long centuries of suffering, was about to set an example of how to restore the dignity of man. Awolowo, the leader of the opposition party in Nigeria, claimed that the final battle for the 'respect of the negro' would be fought and won in Africa. They were both confident that all Africans were of the same opinion (Segal 1962: 229). Soyinka, on the other hand, warned not of white racism, but of 'black inhumanity':

> The Angolan or the South African writer [. . .] sees, and he under-stands for the first time that, given equal opportunity, the black tin god a few thousand miles to the north of him would degrade and dehu-manize his victim as capably as Vorster or Governor Wallace. This fact has been ever-present, this knowledge is not new, and the only wonder is that the *romancier*, the intellectual myth-maker, has successfully deleted this black portion of a common human equation. And the intermittent European exercises in genocide have been duplicated on the African continent admittedly on a lower scale, but only because of the temporary lack of scientific organization. We, whose humanity the poets celebrated before the proof, whose lyric innocence was daily questioned by the very pages of the newspapers, are now being forced by disaster, not foresight, to a reconsideration of our relationship to the outer world. It seems to me that the time has now come when the African writer must have the courage to determine what alone can be salvaged from the recurrent cycle of human stupidity. The myth of irrational nobility, of a racial essence that must come to the rescue of white depravity, has run its full course. It never in fact existed, for this was not the problem but the camouflage. And it has become important to state this because the old camouflage has begun lately to take on a new camouflage of fresh understanding. The movement which began with the war-cry of cultural separatism, modified itself with an acknowledgement of historical expediency of the revolt – I refer, of course, to *Négritude* – has found a latter-day succession in a call to be the bridge, to bring about the salvation of the world by a marriage of abstractions. It is a remarkable fact that the European writer, who had both the leisure and the long history of introspection to ascertain his spiritual needs, has not yet sent out a call to the black writer for rescue. Surely the game is transparent by now; the writer's philosophy does not prescribe from his own society, his enlargement of commitment

conveniently ignores his own inadequacies, overlooking the well-tried
adage which cautions very simply, 'Physician heal thyself'.

(Soyinka 1998: 19)

Soyinka was acutely aware of the intellectual difficulties of the post-colonial
context and in 1971 addressed a UNESCO meeting on the subject of finding an acceptable literary language for independent Africa to replace the
tainted power structures of the old colonial languages. The issue, he said,
was beyond culture:

> I say it is beyond culture because it has become a weapon for the
> preservation of an artificial elite which feeds on the ritual of diplomatic
> education; it is used as a criterion for determining which acolytes shall
> be charged with the formulation of new minds.

(Soyinka 1971: 4)

For Soyinka it was important to see Africa in very realistic terms.

Soyinka, African writers and Negritude

Soyinka has dissected the African-ness of writers like Mongo Beti, Camara
Laye, Chinua Achebe, Alex La Guma, Peter Abrahams, Leopold Sedar Senghor, Christopher Okigbo, Lewis Nkosi and William Conton – all of whom
were to some degree influenced by Negritude. In doing so he has questioned
not only their common African backcloth, but the moral and artistic integrity
of their work. Soyinka found that much African literature was written for a
European audience, and that the creative idioms of 'western literature' had
been imperfectly assimilated to produce peculiar hybrids like Camara Laye's
The Radiance of the King, or poetry which set out to rework the image clusters
of Ezra Pound and T. S. Eliot around what Soyinka termed 'the oil bean
and the naked spear'. He believed that much of the poetry that came out of
the Negritude movement was very poor. He took the critic Adrian Roscoe to
task for saying that it was necessary to take badly written poetry seriously
simply because it pointed out a political, social and ideological crossroads, a
'certain phase of Negritude'. He singled out a poem by Mabel Segun as an
example of poetry that, while it was acceptable within the terms of Negritude, was lamentable in every other way:

> Here we stand
> infants overblown
> poised between two civilizations
> finding the balance irksome

itching for something to happen
to tip us one way or the other
groping in the dark for a helping hand
and finding none.
I'm tired, O my God, I'm tired
I'm tired of hanging in the middle way –
but where can I go?

(Soyinka 1976: 130)

Soyinka praised Birago Diop's work as much for its honesty as for the rarity of that honesty within the literature of Negritude. Soyinka insisted that the prophets of Negritude, by praising 'truly African values', had often unwittingly reduced African literature to a burnt offering – 'charred skin on a defiant platter':

> It is futile now to knock Negritude; it is far more useful to view it as a historical phenomenon and to preserve the few truly creative pieces that somehow emerged in spite of the philosophical straightjacket. But it is not so easy to ignore the facile exploiters of the fallacy, since they, even more than the muscular emblem bearers of Negritude, have been welcomed most readily into the bosom of the foreign critic.

(Soyinka 1998: 8)

Negritude, Soyinka claimed, was created out of a tragic loss: however, the opportunity of becoming European had never existed, nor was it possible for Africans to shed their culture and background. What was on offer, he said, was merely 'one of the unfortunate by-products of Negritude, the abysmal angst of low achievement'. Negritude, he said, for the purpose of cultural retrieval, was 'a kind of pastoral idyllism' which could only be the first phase of recovery from the realities of post-colonial Africa.

Soyinka also managed to upset a great many people with his comments on the supposed brotherhood between the African world and the Muslim world, and their shared heritage of struggle against Europe. In reviewing Yambo Oulouguem's French-language novel *Bound to Violence*, Soyinka pointed out that far from being beneficial, Islamic incursions into Africa had been 'corrupt, vicious, decadent, elitist and insensitive', and that given the rivalry between Islam and Christianity for the African soul, what was left to the Africans was 'an immense historic vacuum' where the intrusion of Europe was easily condemned, but where 'the alternative candidate for stuffing up the cultural black hole of the continent is yet another rubble maker of cultural edifices'. Soyinka lamented that in ancient times 'Semites' (he meant the word in its widest sense) had been the overlords in Africa, while the 'negro-Africans' had been viewed only as potential slave material. Soyinka also insisted that in early slave trade records, Africans made no distinction between Arabs and Europeans – both were referred to as white. He lamented that it was still necessary to point this out, but that such 'deck-clearing' was necessary before the 'huge labor of retrieval' could commence (Soyinka 1976: 97).

Criticism of Negritude has often provoked cries of racism or Uncle Tomism. Senghor clearly made it a matter of race-loyalty when he said: 'It is just as if Arabs said Arabism was out of date, the Americans that Free Enterprise was out of date, and the Soviets said the same about Communism. In my opinion, renouncing Negritude is a sort of inferiority complex' (Dathorne and Feuser 1969: 336). Soyinka's criticisms did little to endear him to the emerging revolutionary black left. Obi Egbuna, a Nigerian Marxist involved in the British Black Power movement, wrote of Soyinka: 'He ridicules Senghor's Negritude with "tigeritude". No wonder he is the Nigerian wonder boy on the western pop-literature chart' (Egbuna 1968: 8). Chinweizu dismissed Soyinka's poetry as 'obscurantist and indecipherable', a 'specimen of Hopkins' Disease', an 'orgy of self-contempt', 'pandering to the blancophilia and negrophobia of western racism', 'excellent *African Literature* as academics understand the term':

> The author of this confessional poem, though black, is so thoroughly Euro-assimilated that he responds to black and white with the impulses of a white racist! Vorster, Botha, Hitler and other white racists would be flattered to read the poem, and would gladly hail the poet as an auxiliary Bantu spokesman for white supremacy.
>
> (Chinweizu 1988: xxv–xxvi)

African reality

Soyinka was right. With monotonous insistence Africa failed to live up to the dreams of independence and the propaganda of success. In 1960 thirteen African states received independence as democracies: by 1970 only two of these had not fallen to military rule. In the years 1963–8 there were thirty-nine military coups in the independent states of Africa. As if to confirm Soyinka's worst fears about African capacities, in 1967 the Biafran war broke out over social, racial, religious and tribal tensions within oil-rich Nigeria. The bloody and insane rule of Uganda's Idi Amin left little magic in African political life. In the period 1992–3 there were armed conflicts in Western Sahara, Liberia, Angola, South West Africa, South Africa, Zaire, Kenya, Uganda, Somalia, Sudan, Eritrea and Chad, genocide and 'ethnic cleansing' in Burundi and Rwanda, drought and famine in

Ethiopia and 'the horn' of Africa. Even the end of apartheid was marred by tribal violence.

It is not, as racist opinion might suggest, that Africans are inherently incapable of ruling themselves, but simply that post-colonial Africa developed in conditions far from any African's choosing: also that the problems facing Africa – declining world markets for staple crops, high infant mortality, tribalism, entrenched corruption – have always demanded a much more realistic look at politics than the ideology of Negritude could muster. For Soyinka, Africans remain stubbornly as greedy, venal and murderous as the rest of the world.

Negritude continues to arouse 'more than a mere semantic interest' among later generations of African and African-American writers and intellectuals (Soyinka 1976: 126). Negritude fed directly into the Harlem renaissance of the 1950s, and indirectly into the recognition of Blues and the development of Bebop, Motown, Hip Hop and Rap music; it played a key role in supporting desegregation, the Civil Rights movements of the 1960s and the anti-Vietnam war movement; in the 1970s it became the official ideology of the Black Panthers and the Black Power Movement. In the 1980s Negritude influenced the Black Consciousness Movement in South Africa and became a tenet of faith for the extremist APLA (armed wing of the Pan-African Congress); in the 1990s it became a key part of the ideology of the Nation of Islam.

Soyinka has never rejected the main arguments of Negritude in asserting an African contribution to the world. He has rejected only its racist manifestations and its simplifications. He still asks: how is it possible to move beyond a world view constructed out of warring elements? How is it possible to discover a world view that is not racist, coercive or limited, which believes that the Irish are Irish, not Africans in disguise, that Africans are Africans, not children? He also asks whether humans can move beyond a national or local identity, abandon exclusive ceremonies built on chauvinism and insecurity, reject posture and display, and embrace the cultural content of difference. He gave the poets and politicians of Negritude a hard time because he saw them as unwitting traducers of Africa.

For all his long argument with it, Soyinka drew a great deal from Negritude. He has always been keen to share the 'exquisite nuggets of lyric celebration' to be found in the poetry of Negritude (Soyinka 1976: 131). It is worth pondering to what degree his insistence on a unified animistic world, his sense of tragedy, his use of Yoruba mythology as a contrast to the 'logic' of European thought and his yearning for some form of African political unity are akin to Negritude's insistence on emotion, intuition and a non-European understanding of how the world works and grow from the same roots and frustrations as Negritude. Soyinka still insists on Negritude's authentication of the black presence in the world, and emphasizes Senghor's 'Muse of Forgiveness'. Soyinka's loud anguish, however, and his determined political combativeness continue to distance him from any but the harshest critical realism when speaking of Africa, its rulers, its people, its place in the world and the responsibilities of its writers.

13 Witches of Croatia

Dubravka Ugrešić, *The Culture of Lies*

The death of Yugoslavia saw new national leaderships determined to break up old loyalties and to police the borders of the newly emerging identities. In that crisis writers were often called upon to support behaviour they found repugnant.

This chapter looks at the experience of Croat writer Dubravka Ugrešić, who felt compelled to speak as her conscience, loyalty and sense of her on identity told her, not as the new nationalist leadership wanted.

This chapter also revisits issues of loyalty, identity, political correctness, power politics and the duties of citizenship.

The Balkans and Yugoslavia

Since earliest times the Balkans has had a rich cultural mix, a complex pattern of ethnic settlement and a volatile tribal mentality. The ancestors of the South Slavs arrived in the Balkans, probably from the southern Ukraine, in the sixth and seventh centuries. As they did, the major linguistic divisions in the Southern Slavonic language group emerged. South-Eastern Slavonic would develop into Bulgarian and Macedonian, while South-Western Slavonic would be the basis of Slovene and the range of accents and dialects that would eventually be known as Serbo-Croat (Comrie 1990). The Croats accepted Catholicism, but Serbia and Montenegro accepted Orthodox Christianity and the Cyrillic alphabet from the Greeks.

In 1389 the Turks defeated the Serbs and came to occupy Bosnia and Herzegovina. They never managed to occupy Croatia; but south of Belgrade they controlled everything until 1878. After this Serbia became an independent state. However, the Turks did not leave Macedonia until 1912. By then the areas of what was to become Yugoslavia had developed very different cultures based on whether they had been ruled by Venice,

Austria-Hungary or the Ottoman Turks. Yugoslavia was united as one state in 1918, and was declared a socialist state in 1943, while it was still occupied by the Nazis. Yugoslavia could also be seen as divided into two areas of cultural involvement and external influence: the Byzantine–Greek–Turkish–Slav inheritance in the south and east; and the Latin–Germanic–Italian inheritance in the north and along the seaboard. The different federal states of Yugoslavia prospered, but they progressed at different speeds and under different conditions. This complex history means that the lines dividing Europe into east and west, Orthodox and Catholic, Muslim and Christian, run more or less along the Croat–Serbian and Bosnian–Serbian borders (Namier 1962; Taylor 1964; Clissold 1966; Wiskemann 1973; Okey 1986).

After 1945 there were three major religious groups in Yugoslavia: Orthodox, Muslim and Catholic; the Jewish population had largely been killed by the Nazis. There were large ethnic and linguistic minorities of Romanies, Italians, Bulgarians, Hungarians, Romanians, Greeks and Albanians. The three main modern literary languages of Yugoslavia were: Slovene, Macedonian and Serbo-Croat. Although other languages were spoken and encouraged, Serbo-Croat was the main language and the major literary language, spoken by over 17,000,000 people. Serbo-Croat had two major dialects. Sometimes the differences between them were those of accent, e.g. the word for snow: *snijeg – sneg*. But at other times the differences were those of dialect, e.g. bread: *kruh – hleb*, or train: *vlak – voz*. Predictably loan words from German, Latin and Czech are more common in the west, and borrowings from Turkish, Greek and Russian are more common in the east. The differences were emphasized by the fact the Croats used the Latin alphabet, while Serbs used Cyrillic.

Yugoslav culture

Although Yugoslav literature traces its origins back to a huge body of ancient Balkan songs and poems, closely connected to the Homeric oral tradition of ancient Greece, the Turkish occupation put a stop to almost all literary and cultural development in Serbia, Macedonia and Bosnia and meant a huge cultural discontinuity. For all those who fell under Turkish rule this was five hundred years of cultural emptiness. Even to the casual observer the legacy of the Ottoman Empire is everywhere in evidence, in mosques and fountains, the national taste for sweet black coffee, kebabs (*cevapcici*) and pastries. But many also see this legacy as deep seated and damaging. Although the Turks forcibly converted many of the local population to Islam, they had little real cultural influence on the people whose lands they occupied – except, by their brutality, to cultivate the spirit of resistance, rebellion and aggressive nationalism. Many, particularly in Bosnia and Kosovo, accepted Islam, but many others refused and migrated to the Austro-Hungarian Empire. The Austro-Hungarians granted these people land along the Ottoman borders precisely because, after their suffering under the Turks, these *grenzer* (border people) were fiercely opposed to anything Turkish and would resist further incursions with their lives.

The effect of the Turkish occupation can be traced in Yugoslav writing and in the mind sets of intellectuals. Critics point out that it is difficult to speak of a single 'Yugoslav' literature. Many Serbian and Macedonian writers now see their task as boring a hole through from the fourteenth century to the present – that is in creating a modern literary culture which is something more than a stultified survivalist folk culture, dealing in peasant colloquialisms and agricultural norms. Croat writers, on the other hand, simply because they are not struggling with a Turkish legacy, have been much more clearly tied to European developments and trends. Croatia was never occupied by the Turks and had been able to take part in the European Renaissance, was closely tied to Slovenia and the intellectual climate of Austria-Hungary, and had enjoyed a cultural flowering in the nineteenth century (Johnson 1970).

Yugoslav socialism

From 1945 the communist leader Tito ruled Yugoslavia in a delicate balancing act. In the main he attempted to keep the numerically superior Serbs from dominating the army, party, government, educational institutions and individual republics. In 1948 Yugoslavia was expelled from the Soviet bloc, and was thus spared the worst excesses of the Stalinist era. It developed as an independent federal socialist state, and compared to the states of the eastern bloc was far more relaxed and far more prosperous than many could have hoped. In a country that was still predominantly rural, cultural and intellectual life was mainly restricted to Skopje, Sarajevo, Ljubljana, Novi Sad, Zagreb and Belgrade. Commenting on his visit in 1963 the English literary critic Alvarez observed:

> The streets of Belgrade are full of leather faced peasants in felt boots, shawls, skull caps and sheepskin jackets. Granted that there has been a big shift of population into the towns in the last few years; before the war seventy-five percent of the population was non-urban, now only fifty per cent is. Yet the peasants of Belgrade, too numerous to be casual visitors, seem untouched by town habits and dress. [. . .] This split is everywhere; you are aware of it from the moment you arrive [. . .] on the one side is primitivism: the centuries old tradition of those

oral folk epics which are still sung in the mountains; the bitter but now successful battle against illiteracy. On the other is the highly cosmopolitan, Europeanized sophistication of the urban writers.

(Alvarez 1965: 91)

The traditional animosity between Serbs and Croats was suspended in 1945 mainly because Tito insisted on dissolution of *all* national and religious rights, in order to gather everyone into the new postwar communist Yugoslav identity. Although literature was still a battlefield between intellectuals and the Party, there was very little state censorship. In the 1960s Zamyatin's *We*, Orwell's *1984*, Pasternak's *Dr Zhivago* and Solzhenitsyn's *Cancer Ward* and *First Circle* were all translated and published openly in Yugoslavia (Fejto 1974). This meant that writers were able to operate in a market where they were judged mainly on aesthetic rather than political grounds. It also meant that as no official culture was ever really established, there was no effective literary or intellectual opposition. However, this did not mean that politics did not impinge on the writers or their work. In fact self-censorship could, in its own way, be just as crippling in its own way as state censorship (Kiš 1995: 89). However, Tito, the Party and the Yugoslav state had only addressed surface issues in Yugoslavia. Animosity between the factions, religions, languages and identities was not addressed but simply repressed. Dubravka Ugrešić, for example, has described the environment in which she grew up:

> Bulgarians were 'black' (Crni Bugari), Gypsies were stealing small children, Serbs were primitive barbarians, Gypsies in a word, Croats were all 'faggots', Muslims had six toes-fingers and were all dummies, Italians ate live cats, Montenegrins were not people but turtles, that's how lazy they were, male Slovenians were all suckers, joddlers, while female Slovenians were 'girls with round heels', 'slots' [*sic*].
>
> (Ugrešić n.d.)

Ugrešić and Yugoslav literature

Dubravka Ugrešić, possibly 'the greatest contemporary Croatian writer', was born in 1949 in a small town near Zagreb, the main city of Croatia (Hawksworth 1997). She remembers tasting her first orange and receiving her first doll, both at the age of five. At her primary school, where she started in 1957, her reading primer distributed Croat and Serbian names roughly equally, gave rules for life, advice about currency and holidays and did not shy from showing both Latin and Cyrillic alphabets. Ugrešić, after graduation, worked at the Institute for Literary Scholarship at the

University of Zagreb, writing and translating extensively on the culture of the Russian avant-garde.

As the crisis in Yugoslav life became worse she turned increasingly to her own writing – novels, short stories and essays. Her stories have been translated into several languages. She has also written screenplays for TV and film. Her screenplay of her novel *In the Jaws of Life and Other Stories* (1981) won an award as the best Yugoslav film of 1984. She also published *Fording the Stream of Consciousness* (1988), and was awarded the prestigious Charles Veillon European Essay Prize in 1996, and the Dutch Verseprijs (Artist in Resistance Prize) in 1997 for *The Culture of Lies* (1998). She has also published *The Museum of Unconditional Surrender* (1997), which became a bestseller in Germany, and has contributed to *The Times Literary Supplement, Die Zeit* and *Lettre Internationale*.

Ugrešić described the main difference between the situation of the writer in Yugoslavia and that prevailing in other east European states:

> Contemporary Yugoslav literatures were free of imposed aesthetic ideological norms. After diplomatic relations with the Soviet Union were broken off in 1948 [. . .] the door to normative socialist-realism and the import of Soviet culture was closed, without ever really having opened. There were, of course, forbidden topics, but they were never part of a system of aesthetic and ideological norms. And then, those restrictions were soon lifted, the taboos revoked, and in 1971 in Croatia we saw that there was only one serious veto: nationalism.
>
> (Ugrešić 1998: 37)

By and large Yugoslav writers had been freed from the burden of national conscience that bothered Russian and Polish writers under communism, but also, under Yugoslav socialism, had been freed from the burden of writing for a strictly commercial market.

> Because it was only in a wild, non-commercial, disorganized and unarticulated culture that astonishing un-provincial gestures could occur, such as the abundant translation of books which could not have been translated in other, commercially oriented cultures. It was only in that confused, half-literate and at the same time highly literate culture, that our own books could be printed in lavish bindings. Only in an extravagant, crazy country between communism and capitalism [. . .] could books be printed whose costs could not be covered by sales, the expense of whose production exceeded their price. From an entirely literary point of view, the Yugoslav writer lived like a rich pauper. The contemporary Yugoslav writer lived in a literary centre oriented

to and open to the *West*, but at the same time open to all the different centers within Yugoslavia. The Yugoslav cultural space was shared, it was made up of different cultural and linguistic traditions which blended and communicated with one another. In practice, for the Yugoslav writer who knew the literatures of the Yugoslav peoples, both the Latin and the Cyrillic ones, that meant living in Zagreb and having publishers in Belgrade, readers in Ljubljana, Sarajevo, Skopje and Pristina. It meant freely living different cultures and experiencing them all as one's own.

(Ugrešić 1998: 38)

The problems became apparent only with Tito's death in 1980. In the postwar period the Serbs had found a substitute for the independent Serbian state they had lost under the Turks in the monolithic and Byzantine structure of the Communist Party. The Yugoslav state came to resemble the map of Greater Serbia that many Serbian nationalists carried round in their heads. Serbs had come to dominate not only the Serbian Communist Party, but the Croat and Bosnian bureaucracy and the Croatian Communist Party. While the other nationalities were keen to get out from under Serbian dominance, the Serbs were not prepared to relinquish their hold on their Greater Serbian version of Yugoslavia.

Cultural transition

By the late 1980s, while it was not rich, Yugoslavia had achieved economic security and had enjoyed political stability for over forty years: it had a federal government, six republican and two provincial governments, and no less than ten communist parties – one for each of the governments, a federal party and one for the army. In spite of the difficulties, Yugoslavia was in fact well set up to make the transition from one-party state to multiparty democracy, from semi-planned economy to free market capitalism. However, Yugoslavs made a mistake in the 1980s when they allowed politicians to form political parties along national and ethnic lines, as these formed the basis for a revival of the very things that Tito had fought long and hard to suppress (Glenny 1992; Silber and Little 1995). By the late 1980s the rulers of Yugoslavia had little to gain from such a transition. They had a great deal more to retain by exciting ethnic problems. Politicians of all kinds promoted the pipe-dream that ethnic purity and territorial integrity would somehow solve everyone's problems and give everyone a better life.

To start with, the shifting about of the people was carried out in the name of the fine and vague phrase *national homogenization*. Then the popular shifting about acquired an organized administrative shape in the population census. Then the statistically indifferent censuses took on the warmer, more emotional form of voluntary public declarations (I am a Croat, Serb, Muslim, Slovene . . .). New words began to enter the language of the media: *ethnically clean* (territory, team, side, work force), as opposed, therefore, to ethnically unclean ones. *Clean* and *unclean* quickly spread to the *dirty war*, with accompanying formulations (*cleansing terrain, ethnic cleansing*). Every day new maps of Yugoslavia surfaced in the media with differently colored patches; everyone experienced some color and patch as threatening. [. . .] Then, within the clearly designated national groups a new agitation began: people began to look for a new, additional nuance in the brand, one that would place them in a special position, which would distinguish the *great* Croat from the good Croat and the good Croat from the bad Croat, the *great* Serb from the mere Serb.

(Ugrešić 1998: 40)

Multinational Yugoslavia would almost certainly pay a very heavy price for its democratic ambitions. Serbian dominance had led to resentment and at the first opportunity – once they had achieved independence in 1990 – the Croats began to demote Serbs and promote all things Croatian. This coupled with Germany's haste in recognizing Croat independence, without waiting for any assurances on the subject of ethnic minorities, led the Serbs to believe that their 600,000 compatriots in Croatia were at risk. At the same time, speech and literature were purged: Croats began to 'expel' Serbisms and the Serbs began to 'expel' Croaticisms. At one point Ugrešić asked her mother not to talk about TV programmes or actors from Belgrade, saying: 'Hush, mother, they'll say you are a representative of the Jugo-Chetnik, Bolshevik-Commmunist band, a remnant of the former non-national regime' (Ugrešić 1998: 108). Croatia began to rename its streets and squares with patriotic names from Croat history: for example, the Square of the Victims of Fascism became the Square of the Great Croatian Forebears (Ugrešić 1998: 107). The Croat Society of Writers suddenly expanded its membership to include fifty new loyal Croat writers and to elect a president who was an open admirer of Croat nationalist President Tudjman. Ugrešić gives an example of how the culture contorted:

In their zeal for cleanliness the cleaners sometimes use dirty methods. One of these is the collective smearing of the house with collective shit, to ensure that the undesirable owner abandons the house for ever. This original method of cleaning was adopted by the inhabitants of a small island town on the Adriatic. The house in question belonged to a former Yugoslav minister, a Croat. The local police did nothing to suggest that such methods of cleaning were unacceptable. It is itself, after all, deeply imbued with the spirit of the new hygienic slogan. [. . .] Following the indistinct instructions of the Croatian Minister of Culture, patriotic librarians are quietly putting books by Serbian writers into the cellars, cleansing the shelves of enemy Cyrillic, and also of Latin-script books imbued with the 'Yugoslav spirit'. A nicely designed strip, with a folk motif, has appeared on books by Croatian writers. In the future this little sign will distinguish Croatian from non-Croatian books, including Shakespeare.

(Ugrešić 1998: 62)

But Ugrešić, while recognizing that the blame for the Balkan wars of Yugoslavia lay clearly with the politicians, their appeal to populist solutions and their manipulation of public fears, did not let the intellectuals off the hook. By siding with the new rulers rather than criticizing them, intellectuals had helped control the media, dismantle the balances of the old state, promote the power of the military, and produce new 'national' cultures and 'national' art. It must be said that the Croats and Serbs of the rural districts bordering the two ancient identities, both of whom often displayed medieval attitudes and identities, were those most actively involved as 'auxiliaries' in the heavy and persistent fighting from 1991 onwards and were people for whom the notion of culture hardly figured. That much would have been clear to anyone speaking the appropriate languages capable of listening to these people on TV. But the unsettling effect of their identities, fears and personalities worked through the entire society:

> The identity of the writer, the intellectual, is called into question in the turbulent times of the destruction of old values and the establishment of new ones. Some have found an identity, others have lost one. To speak about identity at a time when many people are losing their lives, the roof over their heads and those closest to them seems inappropriate. Or else the only thing possible: everything began with that question, with that question like an unfortunate noose everything ends.

(Ugrešić 1998: 45)

Nationalist kitsch

Acutely aware of the linguistic and cultural complexities that surrounded her, Ugrešić was also profoundly unpolitical in her relationship to these things:

I grew up in a multinational, multicultural and mono-ideological community that had a future. I was not interested in politics. My parents
taught me nothing about it. The words 'religion', 'people', 'nationality',
or even 'communism' and 'the party' meant nothing to me. I only ever
wrote one political sentence (and I stole that from a child): 'I love my
country because it's small and I feel sorry for it.'

(Ugrešić 1998: 5)

She was also aware that in the new situation kitsch played an important
political role:

In a country which has fallen apart, kitsch, as an important element of
that country's ideological strategy, has also disintegrated: each side has
now dragged relevant parts out of the ruins, and stuck them together
in new strategic monsters. [. . .] Although the kitsch of today fits the
old one like a photograph torn in half, the two pictures are different.
Socialist kitsch declared its ideology: brotherhood and unity, interna-
tionalism, social equality, progress and the like. The fundamental ideas
of nationalist kitsch are: national sovereignty and privilege for the individual on the basis of acceptable blood group. Socialist kitsch has a
futuristic projection, and therefore a strong Utopian dimension.
Nationalist kitsch draws its content from passionate submersion in 'the
essence of national being' and is therefore turned towards the past,
deprived of any Utopian dimension. The key symbols of socialist
kitsch are connected with work, progress, equality (railways, roads,
factories, sculptures of peasants and workers with their arms round
each other and such like). The key symbols of nationalist kitsch are
connected with national identity (knights, coats of arms, Catholic and
Orthodox crosses, sculptures of historical heroes, and so on). Both kinds
of kitsch employ an identical strategy of seduction. There is, of course,
another fundamental difference. The socialist state kitsch was created
in peacetime, in a country with a future before it. This other kitsch,
this 'gingerbread heart culture', is poured like icing over the appalling
reality of war.

(Ugrešić 1998: 52)

The masculine war

Ugrešić was perhaps at her most acute in linking these changes and the
war mentality to the pattern of male behaviour in Yugoslavia – and in this
she was scathing. She pointed out that the war in Yugoslavia was 'a mascu-
line war' in which women, raped by all sides, were but 'post-boxes used to

send messages to those other men, *the enemy*' (Ugrešić 1998: 122). For her, Yugo-man was something barbaric, in his natural element only in a bar, surrounded by a pack of other men, defacing posters of women, telling endless 'coprology' jokes, seeing women in only one acceptable role: 'the role of her own sexual organ':

> Women's status is securely marked by language. The colloquial synonym for a woman, and it has a long tradition and wide usage, is 'pička' (cunt). There is another colloquial expression in equally widespread use: 'pizda'. But while 'pizda' can refer to a man, a weak, unreliable person, a 'bad lot' (a man who behaves like a woman in other words!), 'pička' can be used only of women. These colloquialisms are so widespread and frequent that they have lost their offensive connotation, and are used even by women themselves. When asked in an interview for the *Village Voice*, what democracy meant to him, the writer and Yugo-male Milorad Pavić replied that democracy was 'pičkin dim'. As the journalist did not know what this meant, Pavić repeated bravely in his halting English: '. . . A smoke of the cunt!' Cunt smoke is the commonest Croatian and Serbian expression for nothing, for something non-existent. When people who communicate in language want to say something is entirely worthless, they use the poetic image of the female sexual organ with smoke rising from it. If Yugo-man wants to issue a serious threat to someone, he will again think of the female sex ('You'll get it in the cunt!'); if he wants to say that a person was as silent as the grave, he'll say 'He was as silent as a cunt'; and if he wants to boast that he gave someone a beating, he'll say 'I thrashed him like a cunt!'
>
> (Ugrešić 1998: 114)

She points out that rape, as practised during the Yugoslav wars of independence, was not connected with any systematic attempt to humiliate 'their' women, or to protect 'our women', but was simply an expression of the 'general cultural attitude to women in the Balkans, exacerbated in times of war' (Ugrešić 1998: 116).

The ruins of Yugoslav culture

Looking back over the break up of Yugoslavia, Ugrešić claimed that in the first three years of war 85 per cent of the dead were Bosnian, that 4,000,000 people had become refugees, that over 5,000 war crimes had been recorded, that it had been estimated there were 20,000 cases of rape (many more had not been reported), and that a list of 3,500 perpetrators had been compiled (Ugrešić 1998: 197). Surveying the ruins of her culture she commented:

> In all the former Yugoslav territories people are now living a post-modern chaos. Past, present and future are all lived simultaneously. In the circular temporal mishmash suddenly everything we ever knew and everything we shall know has sprung to life and gained its right to existence. [. . .] The newly created states are also 'museum pieces', quotations, and the responses of the newly elected leaders are only references to those already uttered. Like the flash of a hologram, segments of former times appear, fragments of history; from the faces of today's leaders there often gleams the hellish reflection of some other leaders, in such a gleam the swastika is linked to the red star. The hotheads of the Yugoslav people dream thousand year dreams, some fragments flash like reality and then sink into the darkness to yield the right to a brief life to some other fragments. In the territories of the disintegrated country, which was once shared, victims and their executioners, attackers and attacked, occupiers and occupied sometimes exchange dreams, sometimes they dream the same dream, thinking they are dreaming different ones.
>
> (Ugrešić 1998: 83)

Croat culture

Inevitably Ugrešić clashed with the new political elite of Croatia. The state had already commenced a policy of dealing with 'public enemies', including 'the victim's quiet removal from public life, administratively justified removal from their post, public molestation and marginalization not only of the private individual but of his or her professional or artistic work . . . ostracism' (Ugrešić 1998: 101). When, at the end of 1992, her essay 'The realization of a metaphor' appeared Ugrešić became a target for the new Croatian 'National State Culture'. She was vilified on TV and radio, and in the press, she received anonymous letters and threatening phone calls, and many of her friends and colleagues at the Zagreb Arts Faculty turned against her. She was described as a liar, a traitor, a public enemy, a whore and a witch, and Croat President Tudjman, who had once defined Croat identity as 'European, Catholic, cultured, unlike those illiterate barbarian Serbs', publicly added her name to a list of undesirables. She also appeared on a blacklist compiled by Croatian neo-fascists:

> The objects of public campaigns are often women (journalists, writers, artists). In a milieu that has hidden its deeply rooted patriarchalism

behind socialist formulae about equality of women and men, 'democ-
ratization' had brought a new freedom for patriarchalism. In this sense
women intellectuals are almost a 'natural' choice as objects of a media
assassination. Along with female public enemies – who are guilty
because they have publicly declared their anti-nationalist, antiwar
and individual standpoint – some men have also undergone a media
lynching.

(Ugrešić 1998: 77)

Predictably Ugrešić linked this characterization of her as a witch to her
understanding of Yugo-male psychology:

The Croatian case has simply confirmed the frustration of Yugo-man,
this time supposedly transposed to the political level. The witch
becomes the most precise mythic image of those frustrations. The
witch is above all the mate of the Devil (public enemy, Serbs, foreign
powers, the Western world etc.). She is the wrecker of comfortable
male stereotypes, she mocks the male value system and calls it into
question, she is a dangerous woman.

(Ugrešić 1998: 124)

She was not alone in this clash with the new nationalist culture, or in
her exile. Slavenka Drakulić and three other prominent women writers
were named for 'special attention' by the Croat magazine *Globus*. The magazine said quite openly that the lack of national feeling exhibited by these
writers, and their obsession with the victims of rape (Serbian and Croat),
were peculiarly female forms of treachery. One of these writers later found
explosives planted under her house, another had her mailbox shot full
of holes by a Croat patriot, another was beaten up (Ugrešić 1998: 94:
Drakulić, *Woman's Hour* 1996). Eventually Ugrešić, Drakulić and the three
other 'witches' felt so threatened they left Croatia in 1993.

Exile

Ugrešić refused to be silenced by the experience of exile, saying that a
repressive homeland was far more traumatic. However, exile brought with
it new perspectives and a deepening perception of what exactly had been
lost in the collapse of communism and the Yugoslav wars:

At this time, the ex-Yugoslav writer, if he really is a writer, feels a sense
of multiple exile. The contents of his mental baggage are revealed as
the 'drama of non-authenticity'. Even the writers of the new states of

former Yugoslavia – the ones who swear that they have finally acquired their true identity – only confirm the schizophrenic nature of the situation in which they are living. Passionate adherence to an exclusive national identity is just another form of alienation.

Writing some ten years ago about the Central European writer, Danilo Kiš said: 'Exile, which is merely a collective name for all forms of alienation, is the final act of a drama, the drama of "inauthenticity". Central European writers have long been caught between two kinds of reductionism: ideological and nationalistic. Though tempted by both, they have learned that the ideals of an "open society" lie in neither, and find their ultimate legitimacy exclusively in language and literature – the "strange, mysterious consolation" spoken of by Kafka. Dangerous yet liberating attachments: "a leap beyond the killer's ranks". Yet commitment is not untainted by doubt: no one abandons a community without regret. Betting on eternity is as vain as betting on the present. Hence the constant sense of "inauthenticity"'.

(Ugrešić 1998: 175)

Ugrešić puts little, if any, trust in national identity, less in the idea that somehow a nation is embodied in its language, refuses to be overwhelmed by exile, is profoundly suspicious of the notion of homeland, and sees nationalism as the last refuge of the terminally stupid. And yet, the effort needed to break away from what she calls 'the land of blood groups', the difficulty of contradicting so much that was taking place around her is clear. While she may have refused the role of 'national writer', her responsibility as a writer is clearly to say what is necessary, to say what the rest of her society is not saying, to say what her society perhaps does not want to hear. Branded a 'witch' in Croatia, she insists that the wisest decision she ever made was to own only one suitcase and leave home: 'I invested my own money in the purchase of my broom. I fly alone.' Ugrešić now lives in Amsterdam.

14 Conclusion

I have referred several times to the global context of the contemporary writer's work. Globalization, though it initally referred to the rapid expansion of trade and technology, now includes the realization that the world is no longer divided into competing military and economic systems, but simply into rich and poor. Effectively globalization now means Americanization, and warnings about the impact of globalization apply not only to the penetration of local cultures by consumer capitalism, but increasingly to the effects of that penetration on the ecology and environment.

In addition, the rapid improvement in the technical means for the invasion of privacy by the state and the media has meant the belief that anything we do has a strictly private dimension is becoming difficult to sustain. One way or another we are all involved in these things. We are all part of the process, whether we like it or not. This final chapter asks: how do these things affect a writer's responsibilities? What might the future hold?

Clearly, although this book has explored some of the issues within the idea of writing and responsibility, it has not exhausted the possibilities. We can say that we have a responsibility not to do certain things and even a responsibility to do certain things. However, what those things might be will vary with time, place and the writer. The subject goes far beyond the workaday and covers a vast and ever expanding range of applications. It is not possible to offer a simple summary.

Writing is often seen as a retreat from the world. Certainly this is how we have been taught to think of writers, and most writers will agree that there is always the temptation to close things off that do not immediately affect them, to keep the outside world at a distance. However, writing has probably only rarely been a retreat from the world. Writers need privacy, that is clear, but their work itself has a life beyond and outside that of the writer. As I indicated at the start of this book, writing is a private act with public consequences. Václav Havel has written that all writers have only one fundamental task:

> That task is one of resisting vigilantly, thoughtfully and attentively, but at the same time with total dedication, at every step and everywhere, the irrational momentum of anonymous, impersonal and inhuman power – the power of ideologies, systems, *apparat*, bureaucracy, artificial languages and political slogans. We must resist their complex and wholly alienating pressure, whether it takes the form of consumption, advertising, repression, technology, or cliché – all of which are the blood brothers of fanaticism and the wellspring of totalitarian thought. We must draw our standards from the natural world, heedless of ridicule, and reaffirm its denied validity. We must honor with the humility of the wise, the bounds of that natural world and the mystery which lies beyond them, admitting that there is something in the order of being which evidently exceeds all our competence: relating ever again to the absolute horizon of our existence which, if we but will, we shall constantly rediscover and experience; making values and imperatives into the starting point of all our acts, of all our personally attested, openly contemplated and ideologically uncensored lived experience. We must trust the voice of our conscience more than that of all abstract speculations and not invent other responsibilities than the one to which the voice calls us. We must not be ashamed that we are capable of love, friendship, solidarity, sympathy and tolerance, but just the opposite: we must set these fundamental dimensions of our humanity free from their 'private' exile and accept them as the only genuine starting point of meaningful human community. We must be guided by our own reason and serve the truth under all circumstances as our own essential experience.
>
> (Havel 1986: 153)

Writing and responsibility are not narrow professional problems, but part of the basic issues of what writing is, what writers do and what writing does. And since these questions raise issues of language and identity, and are intimately connected to questions of humanness, we also have to wonder what humans are and what they do. Responsibility may be, as Havel said, explicable only as an expression of 'the silent assumption that we are observed from above, that everything is visible, nothing is forgotten'. Call this conscience or citizenship, as you wish, but clearly there is a sense in which writers are dealing not only with words, but also with 'The Word'. Understandably, this brings us very close to ideas of God and the possibility that a religion might define our responsibilities for us. Many writers feel uncomfortable with this and, as Jeanette Winterson wrote, prefer to see the subject in terms of relationship to the past, to tradition and the notion of a 'true artist':

> The true artist studies the past, not as a copyist or a *pasticheur* will study the past; those people are interested only in the final product, the art object, signed, sealed and delivered to a public drugged on reproduction. The true artist is interested in the art object as an art process, the thing in being, the being of the thing, the struggle, the excitement, the energy, that have found expression in a particular way. The true artist is after the problem. The false artist wants it solved [by somebody else]. If the true artist is connected, then he or she has much to give us because it is connection that we seek. Connection to the past, to one another, to the physical world, still compelling, in spite of the ravages of technology. A picture, a book, a piece of music, can remind me of feelings, thinkings, I did not know I had even forgot. Whether art tunnels deep under consciousness or whether it causes out of its own invention, reciprocal inventions that we call memory, I do not know. I do know that the process of art is a series of jolts, or perhaps I mean volts, for art is an extraordinarily faithful transmitter. Our job is to keep our receiving equipment in good working order.
>
> (Winterson 1995: 12)

In Winterson's view responsibility is linked to the place of humans in the world, and she emphasizes that if we wish to continue living in society, we have no choice but to accept responsibility for our actions. Havel's musing on the subject, while it is more concerned with the spiritual dimension, led him to the same conclusion:

> The most interesting thing about responsibility is that we carry it with us everywhere. That means that responsibility is ours, that we must accept it and grasp it here, now, in this place in time and space [. . .] we cannot lie our way out of it by moving somewhere else.
>
> (Havel 1991: 195)

Anticipating the concerns of ecologists and critics of globalization by many years, Martin Luther King Jr put the issue very bluntly, for black and white, male and female, gay and hetero, able bodied and disabled:

> If we are to have peace on earth our loyalties must transcend our race, our tribe, our class, and our nation; and this means we must develop a

world perspective. No individual can live alone, no nation can live alone, and as long as we try, the more we are going to have war in this world. We must either learn to live together as brothers or we are all going to perish together as fools.

(Us3 1993)

Responsibility is the crux of the issue of how a writer is placed in society, of what a writer's function may be. Regardless of the faults of 'the system', if we are honest with ourselves we all know that we are responsible for the state of our own minds, our own families, and our own homes and work-places, for the things we write and the opportunities we create. It is only by pressing home questions of responsibility, by insisting that writing, even when it is part of the entertainment industry, is also more than that, by attempting to clarify the issues – what sort of world-picture this writer presents; how this writer reveals the world to me; to whom and in what way this writer is answerable – that we might hope to have something useful to say about the role of writers, the power of writing, the function of literature, the problems and limitations of the commercial marketplace, issues of fidelity and identity, and the future. Writers have little option but to see themselves and their work in the context of a past, a present and above all a future, and in this context – the long run – issues of identity, nationality and language, even issues of race and skin colour, are part of a narrow perspective. Writers can help us interpret our past and understand our present, but it is our future they will help to shape.

The question becomes clearer if we shift for a moment into a 'post-global' perspective and look at the increasingly urgent issue sci-fi writers have been posing for about a hundred years: if humanity gets off this planet and out into space, what part will writers play in ensuring that we know ourselves well enough not to take our worst qualities and cultural traits with us?

If we as writers do not understand something about the way we live, if we do not consider at some point the notion of responsibility in writing, how can we, as citizens and human beings, people who live in our time, in our place, in our society, understand how our future is diminished or enhanced by a particular book or play or poem? Or, by the absence of a particular book, play or poem? True, these questions are not easily answered, but then, they are not often asked . . .

Bibliography

All references to *The Guardian* may be accessed online at html://www.Guardian Unlimited/archive

Alibhai-Brown, Y. (2003) 'It is an honour to stand among the refuseniks', *The Independent* (22 December): 15.

Alvarez, A. (1965) *Under Pressure*, Harmondsworth: Penguin.

Alvarez, A. (ed.) (1971) *The New Poetry*, Harmondsworth: Penguin.

Amis, K. and Howard, E. J. (1972) 'The novelist's view', in *Pornography: The Longford Report*, London: Coronet.

'Apparatus power' (1981) *Labour Focus on Eastern Europe*, 4: 4–6.

Aristotle (2003) *Ethics*, Harmondsworth: Penguin.

Arnold, M. (n.d.) *Essays Literary and Critical*, London: Dent.

Attacks on the Freedom to Learn (1996) New York: People for the American Way.

Ballard, J. G. (1969) *The Atrocity Exhibition*, London: Panther.

Ballard, J. G. (1973 [1995]) *Crash*, London: Vintage.

Ballard, J. G. (1996) *The User's Guide to the Millennium*, London: HarperCollins.

Ballard, J. G. (2003) 'It's a pantomime where tinsel takes the place of substance', *The Guardian* (22 December).

Bayley, J. (1998) *Iris: A Memoir of Iris Murdoch*, London: Abacus.

Beard, H. and Cerf, C. (1992) *The Official Politically Correct Dictionary and Handbook*, New York: Villard Books.

Bell, S. (1999) *Bell's Eye: Twenty Years of Drawing Blood*, London: Methuen.

Berger, J. (1975) *A Seventh Man*, Harmondsworth: Penguin.

Berger, J. (1984) *And Our Faces, My Heart, Brief as Photos*, London: Writers and Readers.

'Blondes – Jayne Mansfield' (1999) *Arena*, BBC 2 (24 December).

Bloom, H. (1973) *The Anxiety of Influence*, Oxford: Oxford University Press.

Bloom, H. (1994) *The Western Canon*, New York: Harcourt Brace.

Bond, E. (1995) 'Bard of prey', *The Guardian* (28 June).

Boundy, C. (2003) 'A tale of two liberties', *The Guardian* (6 January).

Bourne, B., Eichler, U. and Herman, D. (eds) (1987) *Voices: Writers and Politics*, London: Spokesman Press.

Boyd, A. (1999) *Life's Little Deconstruction Book: Self-Help for the Post-Hip*, Harmondsworth: Penguin.

Brayfield, C. (2001) 'Old masters', *The Guardian* (16 June).

Brink, A. (1983) *Mapmakers: Writing in a State of Siege*, London: Faber and Faber.

Brooks, L. (2000) 'Power surge', *The Guardian* (2 September).

Burgess, A. (1973) *A Clockwork Orange*, Harmondsworth: Penguin.

Buruma, I. (2001) 'America's PC police are the new clergy – and standing up to them is the postmodern version of sin', *The Guardian* (18 December).

Canning, J. (ed.) (1965) *100 Great Modern Lives*, London: Odhams.

Carr, E. H. (1964) *What is History?*, Harmondsworth: Penguin.

Carter, A. (1998) *Shaking a Leg: Collected Journalism and Writings*, London: Vintage.

Censored/Banned: Adult Images the Government Does NOT Want You to See on Television (1996) London: 5th Estate Video.

Chinweizu (ed.) (1988) *Voices from Twentieth Century Africa: Griots and Towncriers*, London: Faber and Faber.

Clark, A. (2000) 'Books: pulp fiction', *The Guardian Dumb Supplement* (11 November).

Clarke, J. (1996/98) 'Interview with Bret Easton Ellis', at http://www.geocities. com/Athens/Forum/8506/Ellis/clarkeint.html.

Clissold, S. (ed.) (1966) *A Short History of Yugoslavia*, Cambridge: Cambridge University Press.

Comrie, B. (ed.) (1990) *The Major Languages of Eastern Europe*, London: Routledge.

Crystal, D. (1995) *The Cambridge Encyclopaedia of the English Language*, Cambridge: Cambridge University Press.

Curry, J. L. (1984) *The Black Book of Polish Censorship*, New York: Vintage.

Curteis, I. (2000) 'From the president', *The Writers' Bulletin* (June).

Dathorne, O. R. and Feuser, W. (eds) (1969) *Africa in Prose*, Harmondsworth: Penguin.

Dick, P. K. (1987) *The Man in the High Castle*, New York: Penguin Books.

Donald, Sir R. (n.d.) *The Polish Corridor*, London: Allen.

Drakulić, S. (1996) *Woman's Hour*, BBC Radio 4 (15 October).

Dunant, S. (ed.) (1994) *The War of the Words: The Political Correctness Debate*, London: Virago.

Dyer, G. (1986) *Ways of Telling: The Work of John Berger*, London: Pluto.

Egbuna, O. (1968) *The Murder of Nigeria*, London: Panaf Publications.

Eliot, T. S. (1953) 'Tradition and the individual talent' (1911), in *Selected Prose*, Harmondsworth: Penguin.

Ellis, B. E. (1991) *American Psycho*, New York: Vintage.

'Empire of the censors' (1998) *UNCENSORED* no. 1, London: British Board of Film Censors.

Evans, R. J. (1997) *In Defence of History*, London: Granta.

Fanon, F. (1965a) *A Dying Colonialism*, Harmondsworth: Penguin.

Fanon, F. (1965b) *The Wretched of the Earth*, Harmondsworth: Penguin.

Fanon, F. (1967) *Black Skin, White Masks*, London: Pluto.

Fanon, F. (1970) *Toward the African Revolution*, Harmondsworth: Penguin.

Fejto, F. (1974) *A History of the People's Democracies*, Harmondsworth: Penguin.

Finch, P. (1997) *How to Publish Yourself*, London: Alison and Busby.

Fine, A. (2003) 'Filth, whichever way you look at it', *The Guardian* (29 March).

Fitzgerald, F. S. (2000 [1926]) *The Great Gatsby*, New York: Penguin.

Fitzhugh, B. (2000) 'To sell out takes a lot of bottle', *The Guardian* (6 November).

Ganzfried, D. (1998) 'Die geliehene Holocaust-Biographie' ('The purloined Holocaust biography'), *Die Weltwoche* (27 August): in English at html://www.stopbad therapy.com/experts/fragments/ganzfried.

Garner, J. F. (1997) *Politically Correct Bedtime Stories*, London: Macmillan.

Gibbons, F. and Moss, S. (1999) 'Fragments of fraud', *The Guardian* (15 October).

Gillan, A. (2000) 'The propaganda war', *The Guardian* (21 August).

Glenny, M. (1992) *The Fall of Yugoslavia*, Harmondsworth: Penguin.

Gramsci, A. (1973) *Selections from the Prison Notebooks*, London: Lawrence and Wishart.

Grass, G. (1961) *The Tin Drum*, London: Secker and Warburg.

Grass, G. (1963) *Cat and Mouse*, London: Secker and Warburg.

Grass, G. (1965) *Dog Years*, London: Secker and Warburg.

Grass, G. (1974) *From the Diary of a Snail*, London: Secker and Warburg.

Grass, G. (1984) 'Interview with P. Brady', BBC Radio 4.

Greer, G. (1989) *Daddy, We Hardly Knew You*, Harmondsworth: Penguin.

Greer, G. (1996) *Slipshod Sibyls: Recognition, Rejection and the Woman Poet*, Harmondsworth: Penguin.

Griffiths, T. (2001) speaking at the conference *Writers in Chains*, West Yorkshire Playhouse (March).

Gritten, D. (2001) 'In good company', *The Radio Times* (29 September–5 October).

The Guardian (26 April 2003).

Hall, C. (n.d) 'Future shock', at html://www.spikemagazine.com.

Hamilton, H. (2000) 'Fastsellers 2000', *The Guardian* (6 January).

Havel, V. (1967) 'Politics and the theatre', *The Times Literary Supplement* (29 September).

Havel, V. (1986) 'Politics and conscience' (1984) in J. Vladislav (ed.), *Václav Havel: Living in Truth*, London: Faber and Faber: 136–54.

Havel, V. (1988) *Letters to Olga*, London: Faber and Faber.

Havel, V. (1990) *Disturbing the Peace*, London: Faber and Faber.

Havel, V. (1991) *Open Letters*, London: Faber and Faber.

Hawksworth, C. (1997) *Garden in the Ashes*, BBC Radio 4 (19 June).

Herbert, Z. (1985) *Report from the Besieged City*, New York: Ecco.

Hobsbawm, E. and Ranger, T. (eds) (1992) *The Invention of Tradition*, Cambridge: Cambridge University Press.

Hoggart, R. (1958) *The Uses of Literacy*, Harmondsworth: Penguin.

Home, S. (2000) '*Whisky Galore* revisited', *The Guardian* (11 November).

Hopkins, N. (2002) 'Why nitty gritty has been ruled a no-no in the police lexicon', *The Guardian* (15 May).

Hughes, R. (1994) *Culture of Complaint*, London: Harvill.

Inside Story, Truth and Lies (3 November 1999) BBC 1.

James, E. (1999) 'Binjamin Wilkomirski', *Medicine, Conflict and Survival*, 15/4 (Oct.–Dec.): 432–3.

Johnson, B. (ed.) (1970) *New Writing in Yugoslavia*, Harmondsworth: Penguin.

Jonson, B. (1875) 'Discoverie XXI', in F. Cunningham (ed.), *Jonson's Works*, London: Bickers and Son.

Kadrey, R. 'Crash video lands on US', at http://www.wired.com/news/culture.

Kanturkova, E. (n.d.) 'Doubts about toleration', in *Literature and Tolerance: Views from Prague*, Prague: Czech Centre of PEN.

Karolides, N. J., Bald, M. and Sova, B. (eds) (1999) *100 Banned Books: Censorship Histories of World Literature*, New York: Checkmark Books.

Karpf, A. (1998) 'Child of the Shoah', *The Guardian* (11 February).

Kettle, M. (1999) 'Race row in Washington', *The Guardian* (29 January).

Kiš, D. (1995) *Homo Poeticus: Essays and Interviews*, Manchester: Manchester University Press.

Kundera, M. (1984a) *The Unbearable Lightness of Being*, London: Faber and Faber.

Kundera, M. (1984b) 'An interview with Milan Kundera', *Granta* 11: 19–37.

Kunzru, H. (2003), 'I am one of them', *The Guardian* (22 November).

Lappin, E. (1999) '"The Man with Two Heads": *Truth and Lies*', *Granta* 66: 8–65.

Lawson, M. (n.d.) 'Institute of Contemporary Arts: Bret Easton Ellis in conversation', http://geocities.com/Athens/Forum/8506/Ellis/bretinterview.html.

Lawson, M. (2000) 'Nothing's new in the world of art', *The Guardian* (20 May).

Leavis, F. R. (1948) *The Great Tradition*, London: Chatto and Windus.

Leavis, F. R. and Leavis, Q. D. (1969) *Lectures in America*, London: Chatto and Windus.

Leavis, F. R. and Thompson, D. (1964) *Culture and Environment*, London: Chatto and Windus.

Lee, M. (1997) *The Beast Reawakens*, London: Warner Books.

Lehman, D. (1991) *Signs of the Times*, London: André Deutsch.

Levi, P. (1988) *The Drowned World and the Saved*, London: Michael Joseph.

Lipstadt, D. E. (1993) *Denying the Holocaust: The Growing Assault on Truth and Memory*, New York: The Free Press.

Maechler, S. (2001) *The Wilkomirski Affair: A Study in Biographical Truth*, New York: Schocken Books.

Manea, N. (1994) *On Clowns*, New York: Grove/Atlantic.

Mann, T. (1968) *Doctor Faustus*, Harmondsworth: Penguin.

Milne, S. (2001) 'Corelli's curiosity', *The Guardian* (25 April).

Milne, T. (ed.) (1989) *The Time Out Film Guide*, Harmondsworth: Penguin.

Moore, G. and Beier, U. (eds) (1973) *Modern Poetry from Africa*, Harmondsworth: Penguin.

Moss, S. (2002) 'Bookends', *The Guardian* (19 March).

Nader, R. (1971) *Unsafe at Any Speed*, New York: Knightsbridge Publishing Co.

Namier, L. (1962) *Vanished Supremacies*, Harmondsworth: Penguin.

Nugent, P. (1996) 'Battle lines', *Index on Censorship*, 2, London: Index on Censorship.

Okey, R. (1986) *Eastern Europe 1740–1985: Feudalism to Communism*, London: Hutchinson.

Orwell, G. (1986a) 'The prevention of literature' (1946) in *The Collected Essays, Journalism and Letters*, vol. 4, Harmondsworth: Penguin: 81–95.

Orwell, G. (1986b) 'Politics and the English language' (1946) in *The Collected Essays, Journalism and Letters*, vol. 4, Harmondsworth: Penguin: 156–70.

Pike F. (ed.) (1982) *Ah Mischief: The Writer and Television*, London: Faber and Faber.

The Power of Language (2000), Manchester: Greater Manchester Police Appropriate Language Working Party.

Praz, M. (1968) 'Introductory essay', in *Three Gothic Novels*, Harmondsworth: Penguin: 7–34.

Protheroe, G. (2000) '21st century sitcom', *The Writer's Bulletin* (June): 4.

Pullman, P. (2002) 'Voluntary service', *The Guardian* (28 December).

Rich, A. (1995) *On Lies, Secrets and Silence: Selected Prose 1966–78*, New York: W. W. Norton.

Rolph, C. H. (1961) *The Trial of Lady Chatterley: Regina v Penguin Books Limited*, Harmondsworth: Penguin.

Said, E. (1993) *Culture and Imperialism*, London: Chatto and Windus.

Saunders, F. S. (2000) 'The Vanishing', *The Guardian* (15 April).

Schiffrin, A. (2000) *The Business of Books*, London: Verso.

Schmandt-Besserat, D. (1992) *Before Writing*, vol. 1: *From Counting to Cuneiform*, Austin: University of Texas Press.

Seaton, M. (2003) 'Publishing's latest gimmick', *The Guardian* (21 January).

Segal, R. (1962) *African Profiles*, Harmondsworth: Penguin.

Shelley, P. B. (1977) *Shelley's Poetry and Prose*, ed. D. H. Reiman and S. B. Powers, New York: W. W. Norton.

Sidney, P. (1999) *A Defence of Poetry*, Oxford: Oxford University Press.

Silber, L. and Little, A. (1995) *The Death of Yugoslavia*, London: Penguin.

Smith, R. (2001) 'We're in this together', *The Guardian* (14 May).

Soyinka, W. (1971) 'The choice and use of language', *Cultural Events in Africa*, 75: 3–6.

Soyinka, W. (1976) *Myth, Literature and the African World*, Cambridge: Cambridge University Press.

Soyinka, W. (1998) *Art, Dialogue and Outrage: Essays on Literature and Culture*, London: Methuen.

Spriano, P. (1975) *The Occupation of the Factories: Italy 1920*, London: Pluto.

Steiner, G. (1996) *No Passion Spent: Essays 1978–96*, London: Faber and Faber.

Taylor, A. J. P. (1964) *The Habsburg Monarchy*, Harmondsworth: Penguin.

'Television by numbers' (2001) *The Guardian* (19 November).

Thompson, D. (1933) 'The machine unchained', *Scrutiny* 2/2 (September): 50.

Thompson, M. (1977) 'An anatomy of rubbish' [1969], in P. Barker (ed.) *Arts in Society*, London: Sphere: 36–42.

Tighe, C. (1987) 'A state of mind', *Planet* (August).

Total Film 38 (March 2000).

Travis, A. (2000) *Bound and Gagged: A Secret History of Obscenity in Britain*, London: Profile Books.

Turner, B. (ed.) (1997) *The Writer's Handbook*, London: Macmillan.

Ugrešić, D. (1998) *The Culture of Lies: Antipolitical Essays*, London: Phoenix.

Ugrešić, D. (n.d.) 'Stereotypes' at www.xs4all.nl~pressnow/about/debate/contribution/ugresic.

Us3 (1993) *Hand on the Torch*, album sleeve note.

Viner, K. (1998) 'Great art from the Terror', *The Guardian* (11 February).

Wagner, E. (2002) 'Pulped fiction', *The Times* (30 December).

Waidson, H. M. (1978) *Jeremias Gotthelf: An Introduction to the Swiss Novelist*, London: Greenwood.

Wallace, N. (2003) 'Strange times', *The Guardian* (29 March).

Wells, H. G. (1977) *Selected Short Stories*, Harmondsworth: Penguin.

Wilde, O. (2003) *The Picture of Dorian Gray*, Harmondsworth: Penguin.

Wilkomirski, B. (1996) *Fragments: Memories of a Childhood 1939–1948*, London: Picador.

Williams, G. A. (1975) *Proletarian Order*, London: Pluto.

Williams, R. (1976) *Keywords*, London: Fontana.

Winterson, J. (1995) *Art Objects: Essays on Ecstasy and Effrontery*, London: Vintage.

Wiskemann, E. (1973) *Europe of the Dictators 1919–1945*, London: Fontana.

Yeats, W. B. (1973) 'Among schoolchildren', in *Selected Poetry*, London: Macmillan.

You and Yours (2001) BBC Radio 4 (7 March).

Young, L. (2003) 'We are all the new J. K. Rowling now', *The Guardian* (5 August).

Younge, G. (2000a) 'Is it cos I is black?', *The Guardian* (12 January).

Younge, G. (2000b) 'The badness of words', *The Guardian* (14 February).

Zephaniah, B. (2003) 'You know what you can do with this Mr Blair', *The Guardian* (27 November).

Index

Creative Writing and the New Humanities

Paul Dawson

'It is rare to have a text that not only meets a very real need academically, but one that is written with heartening persuasion and clarity. This is clearly excellent scholarship.'

David Morley, *Director, University of Warwick Writing Programme*

Discussions about Creative Writing have tended to revolve around the perennial questions 'can writing be taught?' and 'should it be taught?'

In this ambitious new book, Paul Dawson carries the debate far beyond the usual arguments and demonstrates that the discipline of Creative Writing developed as a series of pedagogic responses to the long-standing 'crisis' in literary studies. He traces the emergence of Creative Writing alongside the New Criticism in American universities; examines the writing workshop in relation to theories of creativity and literary criticism; and analyses the evolution of Creative Writing pedagogy alongside and in response to the rise of 'theory' in America, England and Australia.

Paul Dawson's thoroughly researched and engaging book provides a fresh perspective on the importance of Creative Writing to the 'new humanities' and makes a major contribution to current debates about the role of the writer as public intellectual.

0-415-33220-6 (hbk)
0-415-33221-4 (pbk)

Available at all good bookshops
For ordering and further information please visit:
www.routledge.com

Creativity: History, Theory and Practice

Rob Pope

This remarkable volume tackles the theory, history and practice of creativity head-on. Informed by critical theory, grounded in cultural history and rooted in specific texts and contexts, it explores:

- The need to rethink creativity, moving beyond the 'how to' of so much current publishing to a fully historicised, theorised understanding of the term
  The many ways in which creativity has been or might be defined and debates around the issue of definition
- Myths, stories and metaphors of creation and recreation, as well as the creation of 'truth' through myth, story or metaphor in both the arts and sciences
- Examples of creative practices and cultural processes, looking particularly but not solely at the case of 'literature'
- The many faces of creativity, the creative, creation and creators, not only in the arts and sciences but also in fields such as education or business studies, where we might encounter 'creative problem-solving' or even 'creative accounting'.

Creativity will reinvigorate, if not transform, debates around the term and offers food for thought for students, lecturers and researchers in the many related fields.

0-415-34915-X (hbk)
0-415-34916-8 (pbk)

Available at all good bookshops
For ordering and further information please visit:
www.routledge.com

The Routledge Creative Writing Coursebook

Paul Mills

The Routledge Creative Writing Coursebook is a step-by-step practical guide to the process of creative writing, providing readers with a fully comprehensive course in its art and skill. With genre-based chapters such as life writing, novels and short stories, poetry and screenwriting, the book is an indispensable guide to writing successfully.

The Routledge Creative Writing Coursebook:

- shows new writers how to get started
- encourages experimentation and creativity
- stimulates critical awareness through discussion of literary theory and a wide range of illustrative texts
- approaches writing as a skill, as well as an art form
- is packed with individual and group exercises
- offers invaluable tips on style, sentence structure, punctuation and vocabulary

Featuring practical suggestions for developing and improving your writing, as well as information on courses, resources and getting published, *The Routledge Creative Writing Coursebook* is an ideal course text for students and an invaluable guide to self-study.

0-415-31784-3 (hbk)
0-415-31785-1 (pbk)

Available at all good bookshops
For ordering and further information please visit:
www.routledge.com